Stripping
Spreaching
to its
bare essentials

To Heather,
most constructive of critics
and fairest of friends

Stripping preaching to its bare essentials

Simon Coupland

MONARCH
BOOKS

Oxford, UK, and Grand Rapids, Michigan, USA

First published in the UK 2005 by Monarch Books
(a publishing imprint of Lion Hudson plc),
Mayfield House, 256 Banbury Road, Oxford OX2 7DH
Tel: +44 (0) 1865 302750 Fax: +44 (0) 1865 302757
Email: monarch@lionhudson.com
www.lionhudson.com

ISBN 1 85424 712 3

Distributed by:
UK: Marston Book Services Ltd,
160 Milton Park Estate, PO Box 269,
Abingdon, Oxon OX14 4YN;
USA: Kregel Publications, PO Box 2607,
Grand Rapids, Michigan 49501.

British Library Cataloguing Data
A catalogue record for this book is available
from the British Library.

Book design and production for the publishers by
Lion Hudson plc.
Printed in Great Britain.

Contents

Acknowledgments

I must express my thanks to a number of people who have made it possible for me to write this book and made it better than it would otherwise have been.

Thanks to Tony Collins at Monarch Books, for having faith in the project and in me.

Thanks to all those preachers who have inspired and encouraged me over the years, not least my much loved and much missed dad.

Thanks to Andy Wilson, a valued colleague and friend, for reading the chapters in draft, spotting typos and making helpful suggestions.

Last but by no means least, many, many thanks to Heather and Pippa, for letting me disappear off into the study for hours on end when I should have been doing chores or spending time with them.

To all of you – thank you!

Introduction: Stop boring and strike oil

Preaching doesn't have a great reputation. Take, for instance, the definition of a preacher: "Someone who talks in other people's sleep". Or the definition of a good sermon: "An introduction, a conclusion, and the shortest possible distance between them". Look up "Boredom" in the index of either of my books of sermon illustrations, and you'll find that every single reference is to stories about preaching. Like the story of the small boy sitting beside his father during a long, dull sermon who spotted the red glow of a sanctuary lamp in a side chapel. He whispered to his father, "Dad, when the light goes green, can we go home?"

Not that this is anything new. In 1725 James Rudge of Trysull left 20 shillings per year "to a poor man to go about the parish church, during sermon, to keep people awake, and to keep dogs out of the church". In the nineteenth century Sydney Smith said, "Preaching has become a byword for a long and dull conversation of any kind," and the novelist Anthony Trollope wrote:

> There is perhaps no greater hardship at present inflicted on mankind in civilised and free countries than the necessity of listening to sermons. No one but

a preaching clergyman has in these realms the power of compelling an audience to sit silent and be tormented. No one but a preaching clergyman can revel in platitudes, truisms and untruisms and yet receive as his undisputed privilege the same respectful demeanour as though words of impassioned eloquence or persuasive logic fell from his lips. He is the bore of the age, the nightmare that disturbs our Sunday rest, the incubus that loads our religion and makes God's service distasteful!

So should we abandon preaching altogether? Some argue that in the age of the internet and the DVD the whole idea of the sermon is outdated and irrelevant, and that preaching will shortly wither and die. Yet only a few years ago similar arguments were offered about the cinema – and the number of cinemagoers is up – and about books – and book sales have risen! I believe it is too early to write the obituary of the sermon, particularly when anecdotal observation and experience suggest that it is precisely where preaching is held in high regard that churches are flourishing and where it's seen as unimportant that they are declining. I am convinced that preaching – as long as it's *good* preaching – has a future.

Others claim that the centrality of the sermon in church life is unhealthy, and that preaching should no longer be given such a high priority. For example, one recent book argues that "Sermons leave most of us uninformed about our faith. Either we are overawed by the abilities of the speaker and thus left with a tendency to despise our own, different gifts, or else we are repelled or offended by the style and content of the preaching, and as a result inclined to leave." Notice the exclusiveness of that "either ... or", leaving no room to say anything good about the sermon!

As you might imagine, I profoundly disagree. I write as one who believes passionately in preaching, and I believe it can still play a crucial part in drawing people to faith in Christ, strengthening them in that faith, and uplifting rather than "overawing" them. At its best, the sermon can bring the Bible to life and speak a powerfully relevant message from God into people's hearts and lives. It can convict and convince, inspire and encourage, equip and enable God's people to handle correctly the word of truth. In short, by bringing people to God's word, it can bring God's word to them.

That's what I believe good preaching can do. The problem is that not all preaching is good preaching! Elizabeth Achtemeier has written:

> There are preachers who wander from subject to subject, and the congregation has no idea where they are going. Other ministers love to tell very long stories that bring their sermons to a complete halt. Some preachers concentrate so much on themselves that not a glimpse of the Lord can be seen behind their grand persona. Still other preachers despise their congregations and love to dump judgment on them. There are those who commit one of the greatest sins of the pulpit – they bore their people. There are the moralizers, allegorists, psychologists, sociologists, even humanists and atheists – all wasting the glorious

opportunity to preach the gospel to the largest captive audience in the world.

Now, none of us wants to be a bad preacher, and presumably if you've bought this book you want to be a good preacher … or at least a better preacher than you already are … or perhaps, if my publisher (himself a lay preacher) is to be believed, you're just desperate for any help you can get! What the next ten chapters aim to do is to take us step by step from the study to the pulpit, from the beginning of the sermon to its conclusion, offering along the way a variety of tips for tired teachers and pointing out a few traps for the unwary.

It's the book I've been looking for ever since I started preaching over 25 years ago, but haven't ever managed to find. The intention is that it's meatier than other introductions to preaching but easier to read than many weightier tomes; more relevant than many theoretical works and more fun than most manuals. To this end the text will be liberally sprinkled with examples from my own and other people's preaching, jokes, quotations and illustrations. In short, in a book that sets out to help us to be more effective communicators, I have tried to practise what I preach. Only you can judge whether the book has achieved its aims!

Not that I am setting myself up as an expert. I am, to use an oft-quoted image, merely a dwarf standing on the shoulders of the giants who have gone before me, or, to change metaphors in midstream, a magpie who has gathered up all sorts of treasures from the writings and sermons of others. Like you, no doubt, I have listened to some bad sermons in my time, but I have also had the privilege of hearing some very good ones, and had the opportunity to reflect on what makes the difference. I have also had the joy of reading some excellent books and articles on preaching which I have cheerfully plundered for quotations and illustrations. At the back of the book there are some suggestions for further reading which highlight what are for me the pick of the crop. And if I use myself as an example, it simply reflects the fact that, as Thoreau said, "I should not talk so much about myself if there were anybody else I knew as well. Unfortunately, I am confined to this theme by the narrowness of my experience."

I therefore offer this little book to my fellow preachers in the hope that it will encourage you to persevere, both in the study and in the pulpit, and inspire you to preach with greater skill and deeper passion. My hope and my prayer is that God will use it to bless you – and, through your preaching, your congregation.

Chapter 1   # Perspiration and inspiration

"So this is the city of dreaming spires," says a character in Frederic Raphael's novel, *The Glittering Prizes*, as she arrives in Cambridge. "Theoretically, that's Oxford," replies her friend. "This is the city of perspiring dreams." The preacher's study, too, should be a place of perspiring dreams, for a good sermon demands both the hard work of preparation and the anointing of the Holy Spirit – perspiration and inspiration. In this chapter and the next two we'll be looking at the journey from text to sermon; in other words, what happens between sitting in the study on Monday morning with a blank piece of paper (substitute for Monday the day you start thinking about the next week's sermon!) and standing up to speak the following Sunday.

Perspiration

Although I've said that sermons are the product of both perspiration and inspiration, most preachers tend to major on either one or the other, and I suggest that, at the extremes, this can be a weakness. At one end of the spectrum are those who rely on perspiration – masses of it. I have read books on preaching which suggest that the first thing to do is to translate the passage from the original language, then work out the structure, then compare different translations, then carry out word studies, then consult commentaries, then write, rewrite and polish the sermon. It all sounds wonderful, but I think it is an approach that is fundamentally flawed, for two major reasons.

The first flaw is a practical one: a question of time. One of our tutors at theological college told us that every minute in the pulpit requires an hour in the study. It's a great theory, but when faced as a newly ordained minister with two different sermons for Sunday, a funeral sermon to prepare, and a wedding address all in the same week, I realised that there literally weren't enough hours in the day! Even among those of us in full-time ministry, very few are paid to be "preaching elders" alone, and we cannot afford to devote the whole of our working lives to sermon preparation. In the United States, and in a very few big churches in the UK, there are those who are set aside in this way, but when you read their books on preaching, remember that they have full-time colleagues who are doing the pastoring, the visiting, the administration and other such activities that are constantly eating into your sermon preparation time.

The second flaw is a theological one, in that this approach runs the risk of elevating human reason above divine revelation. The implication is that if only we study hard enough and think long enough, we will come up with the perfect sermon. I remember hearing a well known and highly respected Bible teacher speak about the art of preaching. The talk lasted about an hour, but at the end of it I couldn't recall him mentioning the Holy Spirit once.

Prompted by my neighbour, I asked the speaker about this. "I don't see what you're getting at," he replied. "I take the Holy Spirit for granted." And there's the rub. Can we – *dare* we – equate our hard graft in the study with the inspiration of the Holy Spirit? I don't think we can. The fundamental difference between preaching and lecturing or any other form of public speaking is that we believe we are proclaiming the word of God. As Paul says in 1 Corinthians 2:11–13:

> For who among men knows the thoughts of a man except the man's spirit within him? In the same way no one knows the thoughts of God except the Spirit of God. We have not received the spirit of the world but the Spirit who is from God, that we may understand what God has freely given us. This is what we speak, not in words taught us by human wisdom but in words taught by the Spirit, expressing spiritual truths in spiritual words.

Sermon preparation demands a spiritual component. The sermon needs to be grounded in prayer and reflection as well as in textual study, in "words taught by the Spirit" and not just "words taught by human wisdom". Sure, our congregations need to have their minds engaged, challenged and changed, but they also need nourishment for their souls. Words taught by human wisdom can feed the mind, which is a good thing, but only words taught by the Spirit can feed the Spirit, which is an even better thing. How on earth did Paul see that "Do not muzzle an ox while it is treading out the grain" was said for the benefit of us preachers (1 Corinthians 9:9–10)? Presumably he was "taught by the Spirit". So we need to pray for inspiration before, during and after sermon preparation; we need to allow time for reflection as well as for study. In other words, we need not just to read, but also to listen. Obviously how and where we do this will vary according to our personality and our spiritual life. Personally, I find a long hot soak in the bath is a great place for the Spirit to inspire me. Others take a walk in the countryside or have the discipline simply to be still in the study. Some find that absolute quiet is best – others like music in the background. Some want to be away from any distractions – others find that God can speak through the everyday.

Don't get me wrong: I'm not downplaying the importance of the mind or the need for preparation. But it seems to me that too much sermon preparation is simply human activity, no different from the hard work that goes into writing an essay or putting together a talk for the Rotary Club. Let's use our God-given reason, but let's also remember that we're not simply looking for a blessed thought or an insight into Scripture to share with our congregation, but God's word to them. When Jesus preached on Isaiah 61 in the synagogue in Nazareth, he had a word for his hearers for that specific situation, saying, "Today this scripture is fulfilled in your hearing" (Luke 4:21). When we preach on a passage from Scripture, we too want God's "today" message. And for this we need the Spirit of the Sovereign Lord to come upon us; we need the Lord to anoint us, in the study as well as in the pulpit.

One further thought: let's not forget that one way in which God can speak to us is through other people. We know this to be true both from reading Scripture and from our own experience, but few of us take much notice of it when we're preparing sermons. OK, so we might read commentaries or books, and God may speak to us through them (more of that in the next chapter), but have you ever thought of discussing your sermon with other people? If you're in a team ministry, it's obviously easier, as there's a ready-made group. For most of us, however, it's a case of thinking of the right people ourselves. This may be straightforward if we're preaching on a specific issue, as when John Stott addressed major contemporary issues at All Souls, Langham Place and drew together a team of relevant experts to advise him. We can't all do the same in our local settings, but if we're, say, preaching on medical ethics, we can find local GPs and nurses to talk to, or when addressing business issues we can bring in someone from industry or commerce. Clearly this won't apply to most of our sermons, but we can still ask others to share their insights. Perhaps we have elders or some other kind of leadership team to bounce ideas off, particularly if there's something that might be contentious or that we're unsure about. If we're married, many of us can use our spouse, knowing we'll get an honest answer, even if it isn't always the one we want to hear!

Inspiration

If relying on pure perspiration is wrong, then going to the other extreme is equally misguided – doing no preparation at all because, we say, we're depending totally on the Holy Spirit for inspiration. When Jesus said, "Just say whatever is given you at the time, for it is not you speaking, but the Holy Spirit," he wasn't talking about preachers who couldn't be bothered to go into the study, but about those who are arrested and brought to trial (Mark 13:11). The story is told about a preacher who was struggling with his text for Sunday and so kept putting off any preparation with the thought, "I'm sure the Holy Spirit will tell me what to say on Sunday morning." So Sunday morning came and without any preparation he stepped into the pulpit praying fervently, "Lord, Lord, speak to me! Tell me what to say!" There was a long pause. Then God spoke to him: "Tell them you've nothing to say this week..."

The fact is that study and preparation are – or at least, should be – no less spiritual than preaching itself. God should be speaking to us in the study as we read the Bible, as we ponder its meaning, and even as we read commentaries and work out the structure and style of our sermon. There's effort involved, but that doesn't make it unspiritual. If we're going to be a "workman who ... correctly handles the word of truth" (2 Timothy 2:15), we may actually need to do some work! Gordon Fee, a Pentecostal professor of New Testament studies, criticises the popular notion that scholarship and study somehow get in the way of hearing the text in a spiritual way. In his book *Listening to the Spirit in the Text* he writes, "We must learn to do good exegesis ... because we are passionate to hear and obey. This means that we must also be passionate to get it right regarding the meaning of the text – not that God is waiting for our exegesis before he can speak to the church, but because if the text is going to lead us to genuinely biblical Spirituality, we must have the text right so as to have our Spirituality conform to the intent of the text." In other words, if we take our preaching seriously we need to take the Bible seriously, and that means listening to the Spirit *and* the Word. It is going to require spending time in the study: time to engage with the text, which is the word of God, and time to prepare ourselves, as we face up to the awesome privilege and responsibility of "correctly handling the word of truth".

We need to recognise the age-old temptation, as old as the church itself, to drive a wedge between mind and spirit. What God has joined together, let not man divide! Just as we must beware the tendency of elevating human reason over the Spirit of God, so we must also avoid the danger of claiming to be so spiritual that we disregard the mind God has given us. "Be transformed by the renewing of your mind," wrote Paul, and in his letters and the sermons recorded in Acts he gave plenty of evidence of using his mind to reflect, reason and debate. Jonathan Edwards, in the 18th century, wrote, "Though having the heart full of the powerful influences of the Spirit of God may at some time enable persons to speak profitably, yea, very excellently without study; yet this will not warrant us needlessly to cast ourselves down from the pinnacle of the temple, depending upon it that the angel of the Lord will bear us up, and keep us from dashing our foot against a stone, when there is another way to go down, though it be not so quick."

In our preaching we speak from the heart to the heart, we speak words taught by the Spirit to those who have the Spirit, but we also feed the minds of our listeners with biblical truth. Jack Hayford compares preparing a sermon to Elijah getting ready for his confrontation with the prophets of Baal on Mount Carmel. "What I'm doing in my study is stacking wood," he says, "and I'm asking for the fire of the Lord to come down upon the message and the congregation." Another gifted preacher uses a different biblical image to refer to sermon preparation, which I find equally helpful and challenging. Bill Hybels of Willow Creek writes, "Every time I take out a new pad and write a new sermon title with a passage under it, I pray, 'Lord, I would like this to be an unblemished lamb, a worship sacrifice that you would really be proud of. I'm not going to be happy, and you're not going to be happy, with a sick, dying, blind, diseased, ravaged lamb. I will not offer it; you will not receive it.' So to me it's a holy thing to start a new message. If God has given you speaking gifts and called you into the ministry, he expects unblemished lambs." Our sermon preparation is an act of worship, of devotion. We offer our preparation to God, asking his help, his anointing and his blessing on our labours, knowing that there has to be labour before a birth of any kind.

A good verse to sum up what we're doing in sermon preparation is Matthew 13:52: "Every teacher of the law who has been instructed about the kingdom of heaven is like the owner of a house who brings out of his storeroom new treasures as well as old." Each time we have to preach a sermon we draw on a treasury of accumulated learning from days gone by – talks we have heard, personal Bible study, books we have read, other people's insights, etc. But at the same time we look for new treasures, by studying the passage, by listening to others and by prayer and reflection. The process of selection is, we trust, guided by the Spirit as we seek his help. The result of all this perspiration is that, if ever a time comes when we do have to preach without any opportunity for preparation, we won't find, like Mother Hubbard, that the cupboard is bare, but that there will be something on the shelves.

Desperation

That brings me to a different but related question: can we preach an old sermon a second time? The story is told of a new vicar who preached his first sermon on what he said was one of his favourite passages, the episode in the garden of Gethsemane where Peter cuts off the ear of the high priest's servant. The congregation agreed afterwards that it was a fine sermon, and looked forward to the following week. They were rather taken aback when the following Sunday he began with precisely the same introduction: "I'd like to speak to you today about one of my favourite passages in the Scriptures: the episode in the garden of Gethsemane where Peter cuts off the ear of the high priest's servant." And he went on to preach exactly the same sermon as the week before, word for word. After the service there was a bit of muttering, but people agreed that he'd only just moved in, and he must have been busy unpacking and sorting himself out, so they could understand that perhaps he hadn't had time to write a fresh sermon and they'd see what happened the following Sunday. The next week it was exactly the same: identical introduction, identical sermon. By now people were beginning to feel that something ought to be said, especially as the following week was the harvest festival. So one of the churchwardens agreed to have a word with the vicar. "We do appreciate your sermons, vicar," he began, diplomatically, "but we were wondering, as next Sunday is harvest festival, whether you could preach on something topical, something on the harvest theme?" "Of course," replied the vicar. "Just leave it to me." So the following Sunday there was a particular sense of expectancy as the vicar stood in the pulpit and opened the Bible. "My text for today," he began, "comes from the fourth chapter of St Mark's Gospel, at the 28th verse. 'The earth produces of itself, first the blade, then the ear.' And that reminds me of one of my favourite passages in the Scriptures..."

Joking apart, opinions vary on whether using the same sermon again – after a sufficient interval or, more usually, in a different place – is permissible. I have heard some very gifted preachers say that they have reused sermons, while others I know destroy their sermons as soon as they've preached them, in order to avoid the temptation. Speaking personally, I couldn't preach exactly the same message on two different occasions. I believe that the different setting will inevitably demand some measure of different approach or different application. We should be giving people a message for today, not an old one that was meant for people back then. To use an image that I have found helpful: we preachers are stewards of God's word, "whom the master has put in charge of the servants in his household to give them their food at the proper time" (Matthew 24:45). The reheated remains of someone else's meal are not the most appetising (and no, I don't think the Canaanite woman's comment about the dogs eating the crumbs that fall from their master's table applies here!).

There are other hazards with reusing sermons. My father, a retired clergyman, told of a time when he and my mother happened to be at a church in Winchester for the weekend and the visiting preacher was a theological college student from London. The following weekend they were at my mother's home church in Ramsgate, and you can imagine their surprise when the visiting speaker turned out to be the same man. Their surprise was, however, nothing compared to his. He noticed them as he was about to announce the first hymn and was visibly shaken. The reason quickly became apparent: it was the same service and the same sermon, word for word. At the end, rather than go to the door to shake people's hands, the preacher disappeared into the vestry. My father went to see him to explain that he was in the business too, and wouldn't tell a soul!

If I don't believe in reusing my own sermons, then it's probably no surprise that I'm not in favour of preaching other people's either, whether downloaded from helpihaventgotasermon.com or read out of *The Hapless Homilist's Handbook* 2005. Their words are not my words; they're someone else's, and so they cannot come from the heart, even if I think they're written a lot better than my own feeble efforts. Sure, this sermon may impress me, it may even speak to me, but at the very least let me then take its ideas and refashion them in my own words, shaped by my own personality and my own experience. The late Bob Gordon, himself an inspiring preacher, wrote, "Really good preaching or teaching is a spiritual replay on a larger screen of what has already been played on the individual screen of your life. If you don't go there you will never take anybody else with you." In short, don't preach other people's sermons.

If you're still unconvinced, then there's the question of integrity. While I was at theological college, I heard a visiting preacher give a powerful address on the story of the nameless woman who was raped and left for dead in Judges Chapter 19. Months later I was reading in the college library when I came across the exact same sermon, word for word, in a book written by Phyllis Trible. My respect for the preacher, who hadn't mentioned before or after the sermon that these were someone else's words, hit the ground in flames. As that example shows, there's a risk involved in using somebody else's sermon.

My father told me of a minister he knew who used to buy an American preacher's manual every year with sermons for each Sunday. He did a pulpit exchange with a pastor in the United States, and when it came to Veteran's Day decided to use his sermon from Remembrance Sunday the previous year, which had gone down very well back home. At the door afterwards he was told by a number of people how remarkable it was that their own pastor had preached almost exactly the same message the previous year. It turned out that his exchange partner was the man who had written the sermon in the manual.

Having counselled against reusing sermons, I nonetheless believe that there will be many elements of our sermons which have been used before but which are still right to use again: insights we have shared in the past which are still valid and true; stories which we've told elsewhere, for example. I'd be a hypocrite to say otherwise, bearing in mind that I'm reusing illustrations in this book that I've already published elsewhere! We have good precedent for this: there's every reason to believe that Jesus reused pictures and parables and taught similar things in different places at different times. Paul certainly did so in his letters. Indeed, perhaps we could take as our model the two letters to the Ephesians and the Colossians. Many of the same themes recur and many of the same points are made in these two epistles, but each in an individual way, resulting in different messages to different contexts, albeit with common features.

I keep old sermons, not to preach them again, but rather to make sure that I don't preach them again! What I mean is that the same passages and the same themes come up again and again, whether you're using a lectionary or devising your own sermon series. To give the most obvious example, Christmas and Easter come round every year. Because I know I'm prone to think along the same tramlines without even noticing it, I will look back at my old sermons on the same subject or passage to make sure I don't make exactly the same points and use precisely the same illustrations time after time. My wife tells me that nobody's going to remember if I preach the same sermon, but I know to my cost that some people do. Among the guests at a wedding I took last year were a couple I'd married a few months earlier, and afterwards the husband commented on the fact that I'd used the same sermon. It was a fair cop, because the structure was exactly the same, though I did point out that I had changed the illustrations. Even so, I was greatly encouraged by the fact that he'd been listening to my address both times, which frankly isn't always my experience at weddings!

Deuteronomy 8:3 says that when God wanted to teach his people that "man does not live on bread alone but on every word that comes from the mouth of the Lord," he did it by sending manna. But the Israelites could only gather enough manna for that day itself; it couldn't be stored and reused. I believe that our sermons, too, should be fresh for each day. Unlike vintage port, they don't improve with keeping!

Chapter 2 Of making many books

"Of making many books there is no end, and much study wearies the body" wrote the author of Ecclesiastes, and many theological college students would answer with a heartfelt and resounding "Amen!" There are so many books to read, so many reviews that end, "This is a book that every preacher needs on her shelf," how do we know which ones we really need? If any? For a start, there are so many Bible translations: KJV, RSV, NIV, GNB, TSB, TCP, etc. Not to mention the "Wicked Bible" of 1631, in which the seventh commandment read, "Thou shalt commit adultery," the version of 1634 which translated Psalm 14:1: "The fool hath said in his heart, There is a God;" or the "Unrighteous Bible" of 1653, in which 1 Corinthians 6:9 read, "Know ye that the unrighteous shall inherit the kingdom of God?" So the first topic we'll look at in this chapter is Bible translation and Bible translations. Then we'll turn to the question of Bible commentaries, of the making of which there really does seem to be no end. Do we need them? Should we use them in sermon preparation, and, if so, how do we know which ones are best?

Translation and translations

I would say that for absolutely every sermon that's preached from the Bible, we need to start our preparation with the text. For as Calvin Miller says, "The Bible is the book which gives root to the sermon. The sermon is a sermon because it's about the Bible. Otherwise it's just a speech." So before anything else, we must read the passage. Preferably in its wider context, perhaps in several different translations, because the version of the Bible we're familiar with can easily become too predictable. Reading a different version can bring out something new that we'd never noticed before, or occasionally it can bring us up short as we think, "Surely *that's* not what it means?" For example, for some reason it was only when I first read Mark 14:1 in a French Bible that I noticed the irony of the chief priests and the teachers of the law looking for Jesus at Passover time – when people had to get hold of a sacrificial lamb – in order to kill him. These days there are so many English translations around, in book form and also on computer disc, that it's very easy to get a fresh and different angle on any passage. I would suggest that every preacher ought to have at least a couple of extra translations on the shelf, even if we don't read them every week. (You will have gathered that I am unconvinced by the arguments of Gayle Replinger and Texe Marrs in the USA that all Bible versions apart from the King James are the product of a conspiracy between Bible translators and the New Age one-world religion!)

I would particularly recommend the CEV (Contemporary English Version), which has been awarded a Crystal Mark by the Plain English Campaign. The CEV has wholeheartedly adopted the dynamic equivalence model of translation, so that what you read on the page is often very different from the literal wording, but at the same time it is a translation, not a paraphrase, so aims to be utterly faithful to the original. I often quote it in a sermon if there's a difficult passage I want to explain, though I must add that I don't use it for textual study, because it often moves so far from the literal original. Another modern translation well worth a look at in this context is the NLT (New Living Translation), which an increasing number of preachers are using as their version of choice. A thought-provoking modern paraphrase is *The Message*, from the pen of Eugene Peterson. Some people love *The Message*, some loathe it, and frankly I do both! I find that some passages come across with a freshness and vitality that make me sit up and take notice, but others fail to hit the mark, or have too much extra interpretation in them for my liking. In Titus 1:6, Peterson even misses out a whole clause! But all these things are very much a matter of personal taste, and, as I've said, a version that we don't agree with can sometimes be just as helpful in sermon preparation as one that we like.

Then there's the question of whether or not we need to read the passage in the original language. Some of us went to college and learned Hebrew, others Greek, others Hebrew *and* Greek, but lots of us either didn't learn languages at all or learned only enough to scrape through the exams and since then have forgotten the lot. So if you have the ability to read the text in the original, that's brilliant. I don't! But being a linguist by background, and remembering a smattering of the Greek I learned at college, I do find looking at my Interlinear version helpful. For those who can't even get much help from that, commentaries do a lot of the work for you. And although God is able to give just as good a sermon using an ordinary English Bible (or Bibles) and the Holy Spirit, there can be great value in finding out what the original says, in that it can give all sorts of insights.

To give one example, I remember how eye-opening it was for me to read Romans 12:9–13 in my Interlinear Bible. To my amazement, I discovered that there is only one main clause, "Love must be sincere," and everything else in vv. 9–13 follows as a series of participles, explaining what it means to love in that way. In other words, there's a command followed by what it means to put that command into practice. It would look terrible to write it that way in English, but that's how the Greek is constructed. To give another illustration, this time from a single word, in Luke 9:31 Jesus talks to Moses and Elijah on the Mount of Transfiguration about his "exodus", according to the literal Greek word. I am not aware of any of the major Bible translations opting for that term, although Eugene Peterson does use it in *The Message*. But I'm convinced that Tom Wright is correct when he says in his commentary *Luke for Everyone*, "The reason Luke has chosen this word – not least in connection with Moses – is that in his death Jesus will enact an event just like the great Exodus from Egypt, only more so." All this is really useful, practical material for a sermon.

There are traps for the unwary, however, for as Pope said, "A little learning is a dangerous thing." Don Carson outlines a number of these in his very helpful little book, *Exegetical Fallacies*. The most obvious pitfall is to display our erudition by throwing in a Greek word in passing. Quoting the word in the original language may sometimes be helpful, as we have just seen, but as often as not it's just showing off! And that actually puts a barrier between us and our listeners, making it harder for them to hear God's word, rather than building a bridge between us.

Other common errors are to misuse derivations and to mix up meanings. To use a Latin example rather than a Greek one, I have heard it said by a preacher that on the Bayeux Tapestry Bishop Odo is shown "comforting" his troops by waving a cudgel at them, because the Latin text uses the term *confortat*. The moral of the story: we may ask for God's comfort, but sometimes he does that by stirring us up ("afflicting the comfortable as well as comforting the afflicted", in the old saying). The trouble with that illustration is that the medieval Latin verb *confortare* actually means to strengthen or encourage, and doesn't signify to soothe or console.

Another preacher's favourite (I confess I've used it myself) is to quote the Greek word for worship, *proskuneo*, as literally meaning "to come towards to kiss". That is entirely true, but the problem is that in Jesus' day it meant "to prostrate oneself to kiss the feet or the hem of a garment", which is not the way we normally kiss each other today! In other words, it's a term of abasement, not of intimacy. We are misleading people if we quote the Greek word to show that God desires intimacy with him in our worship.

In John 21:15–17 Jesus uses two different Greek words

for love, *agapeo* and *phileo*, when he asks Simon Peter if he loves him. Now I've heard and, yes, I admit it, I've preached, that these words represent different strengths of love, with *agapeo* the purest and highest, and *phileo* the definite second best. The trouble is, those who've made a careful study of John's Gospel have shown that this simply isn't true: for instance, John 5:20 says "the Father loves the Son" and the word used is – you've guessed it – *philei*.

To sum up, we don't need to read Greek and Hebrew for God to use us as preachers, but understanding the original can sometimes give us insights and blessings we would otherwise miss. At the same time we need to be careful that we use these tools properly and *"correctly* handle the word of truth", to quote 2 Timothy 2:15 again (emphasis mine).

Commentaries and other background books

If those who are strong on perspiration make me feel guilty because I don't know any Hebrew and because I can't read my Greek New Testament, I've heard those who major on inspiration pour scorn on Bible commentaries. Read the Bible, they say, and the Bible alone. The Word of God is sufficient! Bible dictionaries, commentaries and the like are "words taught by human wisdom", not "words taught by the Spirit". So what benefit is there in reading other people's ideas about a passage? Wouldn't we be better off simply reading, rereading and meditating upon the text?

As I've already said, there is enormous value in going first to the Bible, working out for ourselves what the passage means, and discerning for ourselves what God is saying through his word for us today. All this is down to us, and nobody else's book can do it for us. We preach the Bible, not the commentary. But through the ages many godly men and women have shared their insights into the Scriptures in commentaries and other works, both scholarly and devotional, and as I said of myself in the introduction, we are dwarves standing on the shoulders of giants who enable us to see further than we could see by ourselves. Again and again I have found that Bible commentaries have opened my eyes to things that I myself would not have seen in a month of Sundays (or in this case, Saturdays!). They have also nourished me as I have read them, feeding my mind and spirit, and thereby making me better equipped to lead and preach.

One of the ways commentaries do this is by unpacking the meaning of the text, pointing out the nuances of the passage that I, with my inadequate knowledge of the original languages, would otherwise not have known. I've already used Tom Wright on Luke 9:31 as one example. Let me give another in relation to 1 Timothy 2:15, a notoriously difficult passage (in the NIV: "But women will be saved through childbearing – if they continue in faith, love and holiness with propriety"). You can see from the number of variant translations given in the footnotes of many Bible versions how confusing the passage is! A commentary helped me to make sense of this verse, so let me share it with you. If we recognise that the preposition "through" refers to difficult circumstances through which women must pass (compare 1 Corinthians 3:15 or 1 Peter 3:20), then the author is saying that women will be saved *despite* suffering the pain of childbearing, as long as they continue in faith, love, etc. It is not the childbearing which saves, but being in Christ; indeed, the childbearing – or, more accurately, the *pain* of childbearing – is something which a woman suffers because of Eve's sin. This not only makes the passage consistent with the rest of Pauline teaching, but also removes a stumbling block to many people's reading of it.

A second and perhaps even more valuable benefit to be gained from commentaries, Bible dictionaries and other such books is that they can shed light on the background to the text which no amount of Bible study by itself could provide. For example, with reference to Matthew 18:21–22, Robert Mounce in his *New International Biblical Commentary* cites a rabbinic saying (m. *Yoma* 5:13): "If a man sins once, twice, or three times, they forgive him: if he sins a fourth time, they do not forgive him." That's a very quotable quote! Or when preparing a sermon on Mark 13:1 ("Look, Teacher! What massive stones! What magnificent buildings!"), I found it helpful to discover that some of the stones in the southwest corner of the Temple Mount are 40 feet long, three feet high and eight feet thick, and weigh about 50 tons apiece. To give just one more example: when preaching about the Massacre of the Innocents last December, it was very useful to know how many members of his family Herod had murdered, leading the Emperor Augustus to comment, "I would rather be Herod's pig than Herod's son!" None of these things is contained in the pages of the Bible; all of them shed light on what is written there. All of them also help me appreciate the text in its context more fully, though admittedly none of them is essential for making sense of the text. Having said that, there are odd passages which are so obscure that light from extra-biblical sources can be invaluable. One such is the prohibition against boiling a kid in its mother's milk in Exodus 23:19; 34:26 and Deuteronomy 14:21. What on earth is it about? (I remember a home-group leader once trying to convince us that it showed compassion for animals, but we were decidedly unconvinced. After all, it didn't make much difference to the kid whether the milk was its mother's or not, as it was dead!) Commentators point to a possible parallel in an Ugaritic text, suggesting that the practice was part of Canaanite religion, probably connected with a fertility cult. I suggest that few of us would ever work that out by ourselves.

I hope I've convinced you that good preachers need good commentaries and other background books. But how do we set about choosing out of the multitude available? I'm not going to give a "top ten" selection, because, as with Bible versions, it's largely a matter of personal taste. The best thing to do is browse in a library, bookshop or friend's study and decide which books you find most helpful. Three useful criteria to consider before getting your cheque book out are:

- the level of detail
- the author
- the price.

With regard to the level of detail, commentaries can be roughly divided into three categories: academic, popular, and in-between. By academic commentaries, I mean the big thick ones, usually in hardback, which are full of Greek or Hebrew words in the original language (for example, Word, Anchor, Old Testament Library). By popular commentaries I'm referring to thin paperbacks which are designed for lay people and usually apply the passage to everyday life (like the *Bible Speaks Today* series or the *Daily Study Bible*). In-between commentaries are medium-sized volumes without too much jargon which nonetheless seek to offer a fairly scholarly guide to the general reader (Tyndale, Epworth, Interpretation, etc). Having made that distinction, please don't think that academic commentaries are all dry as dust, and popular commentaries a lively read. Some of the latter can be thin and dry; some of the former spiritual and inspiring. For instance, Gordon Fee's NICNT commentary on 1 Corinthians is, with its 880 pages, one of the fatter books on my shelves. But listen to this not untypical reflection on 2:1–5:

> Paul's point needs a fresh hearing. What he is rejecting is not preaching, not even persuasive preaching; rather, it is the real danger in all preaching – self reliance. The danger always lies in letting the form and content get in the way of what should be the single concern: the gospel proclaimed through human weakness but accompanied by the powerful work of the Spirit so that lives are changed through a divine-human encounter. This is hard to teach in a course in homiletics, but it still stands as the true need in genuinely Christian preaching.

I know that's rather a long extract to make a simple point, but as this is a book on preaching it seemed a rather good observation to include in its entirety! To return to the main purpose of this paragraph, you need to think what level of detail you want. I personally would go for at least one commentary on every book of the Bible, and ultimately want at least one academic commentary on each, so that I've got somewhere to go to get help on answering *my* questions about what the text means. But it might take some time to build up that kind of library.

Another consideration worth bearing in mind is that of authorship. A tip from a friend who lectures on the Old Testament that I've found very helpful over the years is to find an author that you like and buy everything he or she has written, whatever the series. You've doubtless gathered that Gordon Fee and Tom Wright are among my heroes; we will all have our own. You can also get hold of commentary surveys which give a brief run-down on the commentaries available for each biblical book, with recommendations: Grove booklets provide guides with their Biblical series (for back issues, see www.grovebooks.co.uk), and Don Carson has published a commentary guide for the New Testament (IVP, regularly updated), Tremper Longman III one for the Old (Baker Book House).

Let's be honest, another major consideration is price. Some of these commentaries cost a fortune, and we simply can't afford to buy them all. Buying an entire series can be a cheap (well, the cheaper) option, but be aware that most series are written by many different authors, so the quality may be uneven. If you have a computer with a CD-drive, then considerable, sometimes massive, savings can be made by buying a set on CD-Rom. A number of Bible dictionaries are also available in this format, as well as Bible versions, and if you shop around you don't have to buy expensive packages with lots of software that you don't want and will never use. I'm always on the lookout for bargains, and have regularly found some through Christian Book Distributors in the USA (www.christian-book.com), though postage to Europe is expensive. The thing to remember is that we're building up a library to last a lifetime, and we can add to it bit by bit. In fact, we should go on adding to our collection. Many years ago I heard a sermon by a preacher on a summer pulpit exchange, the sort of holiday where you swap houses and the price is having to take Sunday services. What has stuck in my mind is that the preacher said he could tell the year of his exchange partner's ordination from looking at the books on the study shelves. In other words, he hadn't bought any since leaving college! I think that was a real shame. New commentaries are coming out all the time, and although newest isn't necessarily best, there is often something better than what has gone before: that dwarves and giants principle again. One example is Tom Wright's magnificent undertaking, *The New Testament for Everyone* (SPCK). I grew up on illustrations from William Barclay's *Daily Study Bible*, but frankly the majority are now tired and dated. Tom Wright is aiming to produce a replacement series, and it promises to be an excellent investment for any preacher.

Chapter 3   # Winnie-the-Pooh and the Bible

The way in which I read the Bible was forever changed by C. J. L. Culpepper's seminal article, "O felix culpa!" If you have never heard of it, I'm not surprised, as the subtitle is "The Sacramental Meaning of *Winnie-the-Pooh*". The article begins with Culpepper (who is actually a fictional creation of the author Frederick C. Crews) showing us Pooh's role as Adam: Everyman, or perhaps we should say, Everybear. He demonstrates this from the opening chapter of *Winnie-the-Pooh*, in which we find...

> a story about a certain tree which proves irresistibly attractive to our hero, who conceives a passion for removing and eating something he finds upon it. With increasing pride in his ability to snatch the spoils without assistance, much less with official permission to touch this certain product, he climbs nearly to the top of the tree and – *falls!* (author's emphasis)

Space and the laws of copyright do not allow me to reproduce here how Eeyore, the humble donkey, is revealed as the book's Redeemer and how Christopher Robin is shown to be "God" (as Piglet says, "You'll be quite safe with *him*"). To find out more you'll have to get hold of a copy of Crews' wonderful book *The Pooh Perplex* (Robin Clark, 1983), which includes Culpepper's chapter. (A word of warning, however: after reading the chapter "Poisoned Paradise", a Freudian interpretation of *Winnie-the-Pooh*, you'll never let your children read A. A. Milne again!)

I've quoted this at length not only because I think it's entertaining, but also because it brings out a very serious point which really did change the way I read every text, including the Bible. What Crews shows us is that it's possible to read hidden meanings into anything if we really want to. The technical terms are eisegesis rather than exegesis: reading something *into* a text instead of reading *out* of it. Having focused in the last chapter on the research and development side of sermon preparation, in this chapter we'll look at the production line: how do we go about the work of exegesis while avoiding this trap of eisegesis? In other words, how do we ensure that we are faithful interpreters of Scripture?

I've long been fond of an image used by the nineteenth-century French poet Théophile Gautier, who said that the writer has to "sculpt, file and chisel" to release the "floating dream" sealed in a block, not of stone, but of words. Our task is to unlock the message from the passage and share it with the congregation. Not that I think that there is only one possible message, for God can speak in many different ways from the same text. Nor do I believe that there is an infinite number of possible messages, some of them contradicting others. I am unconvinced by the postmodern approach which suggests that all interpretations are equally valid. As finer minds than mine have pointed out, postmodern writers themselves don't really believe what they say. Their claim that all truth is relative is itself an absolute statement, which according to their own theory is consequently invalid. Their supposed radical suspicion also displays a remarkable lack of scepticism towards their own creeds. So postmodernism carries within it the seeds of its own downfall. Rather than suggest that all interpretations are possible, I would argue that there is a range of possible interpretations. Some interpretations are true, some are, frankly, untrue, and as Calvin Miller memorably says, "The preacher's task is to present the truth in such a way as to make it seem 'even truer'."

Let me give an example from my own experience. In a house group of which I was once a member we were studying a Bible passage – I don't recall which – when one of the members said something along the lines of: "I'm sure Jesus says somewhere that God doesn't like black people." There was a stunned silence as people took this in. Then we tried to suggest in the nicest possible way that, no, Jesus hadn't said or even hinted at anything of the sort. There was no question in our minds that this woman's interpretation of the words of Jesus was different but equally valid. Rather, we believed – and I still believe – that she was just plain wrong.

This may seem an extreme example. But the history of biblical interpretation is littered with instances of equally if not even more bizarre pronouncements. For instance, I remember hearing a member of the House of Lords argue that the Bible shows that UFOs were visiting Israel for thousands of years, from Jacob's vision in Genesis Chapter 28, in which Jacob saw the aliens going up and down the ladder to the mother ship above them, to Jesus' ascension, when he was beamed back up to his people. Dead Sea Scrolls scholar John Allegro was convinced that Jesus was not an actual person but a magic mushroom, and Australian academic Barbara Thiering claimed that the Gospels are really all coded writings which describe the history of the Qumran community. It all goes to demonstrate the truth of "Murphy's Decalogue", developed by Professor Leonard J. Bowman, of which the first three statements are:

1. If anything can be misunderstood or misinterpreted, it will be, and in the most grotesque possible manner.
2. The person with the most serious of intentions is liable to make the most serious of misinterpretations.
3. The more grotesque the misinterpretation, the more tenaciously it will be defended.

So how do we avoid eisegesis in our interpretation of the Bible, particularly if, as said in Chapter 1, we are trying to come up with fresh insights, "new treasures"? How do we make sure that what we're preaching is God's truth rather than our own invention? In the rest of the chapter we'll look at five ways of staying on the fairway, out of the rough and out of the bunkers:

- the context
- the plain meaning
- the history of interpretation
- self-awareness
- reflection.

The context

Originally, the Bible was not, of course, divided into chapters (they were added in 1551), nor written to be preached in bite-sized chunks. We have, however, grown so used to reading Scripture one paragraph at a time, and preaching on a paragraph or perhaps a chapter at a time, that it's easy for us to lose the bigger picture. Modern translations with their paragraph headings don't help! One crucial way of ensuring that we're being faithful to the biblical message is to take into account the context of the passage, by which I mean not only the immediately surrounding verses, but also the context of the book as a whole, and the Bible as a whole.

This can incidentally open up whole new vistas of meaning which we would otherwise have failed to see. For instance, Luke Chapter 20 begins with a challenge to Jesus: "Who gave you this authority?", a question to which Jesus apparently fails to give a direct answer. However, the whole of the rest of the chapter (the parable of the vineyard, the debates over taxes to Caesar and the resurrection, and Jesus' interpretation of Psalm 110:1) provides a powerful cumulative reply. If we were to preach on these episodes one by one, with a week's gap in between each, we ourselves might not spot the overall pattern, let alone the congregation.

Taking the context into account can, as I said, also help us to avoid pitfalls in interpretation. At the first level – the level of the book itself – I always think it's reasonable to assume that the biblical writers were not idiots, and would have noticed if they'd contradicted themselves within the space of a few verses, or even a few chapters. That might sound silly, but you'd be amazed how often widely held interpretations assume internal contradictions. 1 Timothy 2:15, quoted in the previous chapter, is a good example. Even though verse five of the very same chapter states that "there is one God and one mediator between God and men, the man Christ Jesus," the majority of Bible versions plump for the translation, "women will be saved by having children," or the like. To take another equally controversial instance, 1 Corinthians 14:34 says that "women should remain silent in the churches. They are not allowed to speak." That verse has been cited by many a (male) preacher as all the proof that is necessary to demonstrate that women in church should be seen and not heard. Yet a glance at 1 Corinthians 11:5 shows that women in Corinth were praying and prophesying aloud in church without Paul objecting in the slightest. So whatever 1 Corinthians 14:34 may mean, it cannot be used to silence the voices of women in the congregation. The context must inform the interpretation.

This applies equally at the wider level of interpreting Scripture by Scripture. For instance, preaching on James Chapter 5 in a church that believes in praying for healing (as mine does) throws up all sorts of problems and questions. James states baldly in verse 15: "The prayer offered in faith will make the sick person well; the Lord will raise him up." Yet what about those people we pray for who are not healed? Does it mean that we who prayed lacked faith? That the sick person has not confessed their sins? James is silent on the matter, and offers us no help. If, however, we look at the context of the whole of Scripture, we see that, in Philippians, Paul refers to Epaphroditus as having been ill, indeed, having almost died, without any hint of censure because of a lack of faith or unconfessed sin. And when he writes to Timothy with reference to his stomach troubles, Paul doesn't say, "Pray more" or "Have more faith" but "Drink more wine," a prescription that many wish their doctors would give them!

This approach has, I believe, even greater relevance if we are preaching on the Old Testament. As a Christian preacher I am bound to interpret the Old Testament in the light of the coming of Jesus. That's straightforward enough if we're preaching on the forbidden foods in Leviticus or keeping the Passover in Exodus, but what about when we're preaching on the death penalty? I know of respected Bible teachers in England and the United States who argue that the Bible calls for the death penalty in the case of murder. But what about Jesus' approach to judgment in John 8:1–11? Or indeed the whole thrust of New Testament teaching, which puts revenge into God's hands, not ours? Let's get more controversial still: what about the place of the land of Israel in the promises of God? In his book *Jesus and the Holy City* P. W. L. Walker says, "Within Christian theology it is illegitimate to approach the Old Testament text as though the New Testament had not been written," and I believe he makes a very strong case. We remain much more faithful to Scripture if we preach on a text not in isolation, but in the context of the whole of God's revelation.

The plain meaning

In his *Commentary on Galatians*, Calvin wrote, "The true meaning of scripture is the natural and obvious meaning, and let us embrace and abide by it resolutely." The trouble with trying to dazzle our congregations by finding startling new insights from well-known passages is that we risk the kind of creative eisegesis demonstrated in the analysis of *Winnie-the-Pooh* with which I began the chapter. Reading French at university, I was asked to comment on a passage from Flaubert's classic, *Madame Bovary*. Since it was well established that Flaubert used symbolism, I came up with an allegorical interpretation of the scene in question which, to be honest, I myself did not believe. I was given a good mark! I believe we must beware the subtle temptation of symbolism.

Surely no contemporary preacher would interpret the parable of the Good Samaritan as Augustine did, seeing the traveller as representing Adam, attacked by the devil on his journey from the heavenly city. (He further saw the oil as our hope, the wine as an encouragement to work, the donkey as the flesh in which Christ came, the inn as the church and the innkeeper as St Paul.) And yet as recently as 1964 A. W. Pink suggested that the cities of refuge in Joshua Chapter 20 are a symbol of Christ, the sinner's refuge. He listed nine supposed points of comparison: for instance, as the fleeing Israelite had to remain in the city, so we have to remain in Christ. This example alone brings out the weakness of the parallel: the refugee remained only until he came to trial or the high priest died, then he could return to his home. Another area in which modern interpreters rival Augustine in their search for hidden meanings is that of numerology. For example, Mark reports two miraculous feedings by Jesus, the first with five loaves of bread, feeding five thousand men and producing twelve baskets of leftovers, the second with seven loaves, four thousand people, and seven baskets left over. This gives some commentators opportunities for highly creative thinking. Do the loaves represent the five books of the Torah and the seven commandments given to Noah respectively? Or taken together add up to the twelve consecrated loaves of Leviticus Chapter 24? Do the baskets symbolise the twelve apostles and the seven deacons of Acts Chapter 6? And so on. None of these interpreters seems to entertain the possibility that these numbers simply reflect what happened at the time!

Similar but different is the interpretation of Jesus' picture of a camel going through the eye of a needle. I have heard preachers explain this image by describing a low gate in the city wall around Jerusalem called the "eye of the needle", through which only an unloaded camel could pass. The trouble is that there is no evidence at all that any such gate ever existed! Much more likely is that this is an example of Jesus' Jewish humour. Think of the biggest animal you see around you, he says – a camel. Now imagine it squeezing through the smallest hole you can think of – the eye of a needle. It won't fit, will it? (A modern paraphrase: "It is easier for a Porsche to go through a revolving door than for a rich man to enter the kingdom of God.") The plain meaning is always worth considering before we go for a more exotic interpretation.

The history of interpretation

As the illustrations in the last few paragraphs demonstrate, another aid to help us avoid the pitfalls of misinterpretation are the mistakes which have been made, as well as the insights which have been gained, in the past. Looking back over the centuries to see how the church has interpreted a passage not only allows us to draw upon the accumulated wisdom of the ages, as we considered in the last chapter, but also offers plenty of examples of promising paths which turned out to be dead ends. A few of the more academic commentaries specifically include a section on the history of interpretation, but many commentaries include examples of past interpretations sprinkled throughout the text.

How can I resist the opportunity to mention the history of the interpretation of the book of Revelation? More than any other book, the interpretation of Revelation has been characterised by faulty exegesis and inappropriate application, leading to false hopes and shattered dreams. Every generation has projected its present experience back into the biblical book, rather than reading the book on its own terms and applying that to the present. G. K. Chesterton quipped, "Though St John the Evangelist saw many strange monsters in his vision, he saw no creature so wild as one of his commentators!" Thus sixteenth-century Protestants were sure that the Pope was the Antichrist, whereas Catholics worked out how the name Martin Luther made 666. In the next century, the Puritans claimed that the Church of England hierarchy was the beast, while the radicals said Oliver Cromwell fitted the bill. Around the year 1800, some Englishmen thought Napoleon was the Antichrist, while in the Americas it was said that 666 stood for "Royal Supremacy in Great Britain". During the twentieth century the list of supposed Antichrists reads like a "Who's Who" of political and religious leaders. More recently, I have seen "proofs" that 666 = VISA, the World Bank, the worldwide web or even (my favourite) Barney the purple dinosaur.

Again, apart from being amusing, this kind of misguided speculation sounds a powerful warning: let the interpreter beware! If we know the mistakes of the past, we can learn from them. If we see the blind alleys down which past interpreters have headed, we can avoid taking such wrong turnings again. It's helpful to know if a particular passage has been used to justify apartheid or slavery or even genocide. By telling us about such abuses, commentaries and other, similar works can help us to steer clear of repeating the errors made by our forebears.

Self-awareness

One particular slippery slope that leads to the trap that is eisegesis is our tendency to ride hobby horses. Knowing ourselves and our weaknesses can help us to avoid the very real exegetical danger of reading our pet subjects into every passage. For instance, for several years I was sent a stewardship leaflet showing how every single week the Church of England's set lectionary readings offer an opportunity to preach on giving. Hopefully nobody did use it every week, or their congregation would be browbeaten and penniless by now! Equally it is possible, and some preachers see it as desirable, to preach an evangelistic sermon every week, whatever the passage. I'd like to suggest that both such practices owe more to eisegesis than exegesis, or, if you prefer, fail to take the text and the context seriously enough. Because it is clear to me that the Bible contains far more than a message about stewardship and an evangelistic appeal. Before some readers cast this book into the bin as undervaluing the gospel, let me bring in Hebrews 6:1–2: "Therefore let us leave the elementary teachings about Christ and go on to maturity, not laying again the foundation of repentance from acts that lead to death, and of faith in God, instruction about baptisms, the laying on of hands, the resurrection of the dead, and eternal judgment." These are the basics, says the writer, the milk which we need as spiritual infants, the foundation which needs to be laid. Then we must move onto more solid food.

Each of us has different hobby horses. As I mentioned in an earlier chapter, that's why I keep old sermons, to avoid preaching them again. But, equally, we can manage to find the same message in a number of different passages, often without even trying. Of course the same themes *will* come up again and again in our preaching – themes such as forgiveness, adoption, faith, hope, love, fellowship, and so on – because they come up again and again in the Bible. But I am sure you recognise the danger I am describing: that there are a few favourite themes to which we return repeatedly, more often than is justified if we are preaching the whole counsel of God. Self-awareness is an invaluable tool in helping us steer clear of that trap.

Incidentally, there are two other tools to help us avoid

this pitfall before we even get to the matter of interpretation: the commentaries on our shelves, which generally offer a more objective view of the meaning of a particular passage, and a balanced teaching programme. I try to ensure that my congregation gets a regular diet of Old Testament, Gospels, Epistles and issues. This gives them a breadth of Bible knowledge and helps me to avoid constantly riding my hobby horses. For the same reason, I also aim to include, on a regular basis, at least one series which systematically goes through a section of the Bible, rather than jumping from one purple passage to another.

Reflection

So – we've studied the passage, we've prayed, we've read the commentaries, we've avoided our hobby horses and we've written a draft of the sermon. Now we're ready to preach it. Here is where I suggest another crucial step – a pause for reflection where we stop and ask ourselves: Does the passage *really* mean this? Does the text *really* say this? And we must compare where we've ended up with where we started out from, and ask ourselves: Is this exegesis or eisegesis?

Occasionally – thankfully not too often – I have to confess that at this stage, however insightful my thoughts, however flowing my prose, however stunning my arguments, what I've written just isn't quite what the text says. And that material has to go into the pending tray while I go back to the drawing board. Let me give an example. I recently read an exposition of Joshua 1:1–9 which depicted Joshua as facing a crisis. This was the moment when God called Joshua to lead the people into the land of promise, but, the writer says, "I have to believe that Joshua was not so certain." And he goes on to talk about Joshua's insecurities, and how "it was hard for him to see that God had plans for him now." To my mind, that is reading a lot into the encouragement to "Be strong and very courageous," because apart from that command there isn't a hint in the text that Joshua doubted or hesitated at all. It would be a great message on Exodus Chapter 3 and the call of Moses, on Gideon's call or indeed on Jeremiah's, but I just don't think it's justified in Joshua Chapter 1. It's reading into the text instead of reading out of it, and it's the kind of thing I should be looking out for in my reflection on the text before I get to the final draft, and removing.

Now I know full well it's not easy on a Saturday afternoon, or even on a Saturday evening, to have the courage to tear up the script and start again, though thankfully it's usually just one point that needs rewriting, rather than the whole sermon. But if we're going to be faithful to the text and "correctly handle the word of truth", we have to be so bold. To repeat a comment of Phyllis Trible in a different context, there are times when we must be willing to hear the Lord say: "Take your interpretation of this story, your only interpretation, the one which you love, and sacrifice it on the mount of hermeneutics."

Chapter 4

Fruit cake or sponge?
Sermon structure

Research shows that no fewer than 42 per cent of British churchgoers admit to having fallen asleep during a service, over a third look at their watch in church every Sunday, while a tenth own up to having put their watch to their ear and shaken it in the firm belief that it must have stopped! Jokes about boring sermons are legion. Like the child who whispered to his mum as the preacher droned on, "Mummy, is it still Sunday?"

What is it about sermons that makes them dull? True, some bits of the Bible are less than sparkling – the names in Numbers and the lists of proscribed creatures in the Levitical food laws spring to mind. But to be honest, we tend not to preach on those, and the Bible still tells "The Greatest Story Ever Told" even without the help of Cecil B. de Mille. That means it's down to the preacher – you and me.

It could be the delivery – we'll look at that in another chapter. But it could also be the *structure*. Frankly, our preaching is often too predictable. In one of Garrison Keillor's Lake Wobegon books, *Leaving Home*, Pastor Ingqvist is preaching about the parable of the labourers in the vineyard who all received the same amount of money, whether they had worked all day or only a few hours.

Clarence Bunsen works out his own interpretation: you don't need to listen to the whole sermon to get the point, but can maybe just listen to the last sentence or two and still get the message. Are our sermons that predictable? In this chapter we'll look at:

- The need for a structure
- The one-point sermon (the sponge)
- The three-point sermon (the Battenberg)
- The expository sermon (the fruit cake)
- The narrative sermon (the Madeleine, a small French cake, highly significant in a novel by Marcel Proust)

The need for a structure

Every sermon needs a structure. In one of J. K. Rowling's Harry Potter books, a miscast spell accidentally removes the bones from Harry's arm, leaving it hanging limp and useless. A sermon without a structure is equally shapeless and ineffectual, "formless and void". Whether or not the listeners are aware of the structure, the preacher at least should have some idea of it. To change metaphor, if the sermon is seen as a journey – an image we will return to – it may be a mystery tour for the passengers, but the driver at least should know where he or she is going, and how he or she plans to get there.

I have sat through sermons that did not appear to have any planned route or any definite goal, consisting of a series of seemingly random observations and meandering thoughts. The problem with this is that the brain thinks in patterns and looks for connections. Rorschach inkblot tests work on this basis: we see a blob and create an image from it. So do the writers of horoscopes: they know that we attach significance to coincidences and ignore what doesn't fit. Preaching that has no structure but merely follows a "stream of consciousness" frustrates the listener, who is trying to make connections and discern a train of thought. The fact that such sermons are hard to follow makes it all the more likely that the congregation will find alternative occupations, such as adding up the numbers on the hymn board or practising origami with the notice sheet. To return to the image of a mystery tour, unless there is some superb scenery to look at, or interesting staging posts en route, most passengers will drop off to sleep or start chatting to their neighbour. It's much the same in church. David Pytches tells the story of a man who stayed at home while his wife went to church. When she got home he asked her what the sermon was about. "I don't know," she replied, "he never did say!"

So the sermon needs a structure. To borrow some terms from my dimly remembered school biology lessons, it doesn't have to be an "exoskeleton" (ie, outwardly visible), an internal "endoskeleton" is fine. That's to say, the structure doesn't have to be emphasised, as long as it's there. We don't have to begin by saying, "I have three points this morning", and they most certainly do not all have to begin with the same letter! Having said that, it may well help the congregation to have some idea where the sermon is going. The sermon title might give them a clue (though not only are some titles too vague or cryptic to be of any assistance, but I also know that the title I dreamed up three months earlier may bear no relation whatsoever to what I actually say!). The Bible reading may also give a hint, though again there has been many a sermon whose relationship to the reading that preceded it was tangential at best. We may start by stating a question we're going to answer, an issue we're going to explore, or, indeed, three points we're going to consider. It can put the congregation at their ease and help them to concentrate if they know what to expect. I still remember my shock and dismay on my first visit to a particular church when after twenty minutes the preacher was, I thought, winding up nicely, but then announced his second section!

The other point which cannot be overemphasised is that the structure is there as a servant, not a master, and different sermons on different topics or different occasions will have different structures. To give an obvious example, I would not expect to preach the same way at an all-age service, a carol service and a university chapel. There are many different kinds of structure, and each has its own strengths and weaknesses. Each of us will have our natural preference, but I suggest that the best way to keep ourselves on our toes and our preaching fresh is to vary the diet. So let's now look at the four main varieties in turn.

The one-point sermon (the sponge)

The one-point sermon has been championed by (among others) Haddon Robinson in his books *Biblical Preaching* and *Biblical Sermons*. Haddon Robinson is himself an excellent preacher and has had enormous influence, both through his teaching in the USA and especially through his books. In a nutshell, he suggests that every preacher should be able to sum up every sermon in a single sentence, answering the question, "What's the Big Idea?" Everything in the sermon should underline that point, whether inductively, deductively, through narrative or whatever. There may be sub-points, but they are all clearly serving the one main point, the Big Idea.

The strength of this model is clear. One of the guidelines I was given when training to be a teacher was, "Tell them what you're going to say; say it; then tell them what you've said." It provides a clear focus, both for the preacher and for the listener, and thus makes communication easier. It leaves everyone clear about what the message is and avoids possible distraction and confusion.

I have thought of this model as being like a sponge cake ever since a preacher I admired criticised it: "It's fine for those people who like sponge," he said, "but what about those who don't? How can I be sure that every single person in the congregation that day wants or needs to hear my one point? Far better to give them a fruit cake, so that if they don't like nuts they can leave them and just eat the raisins." I can see his point, although to be fair most preachers will sprinkle their sermons with sub-points or asides. Other criticisms can be levelled at it too, especially if it is the only model we use for all our preaching. The first is that it too often assumes that there is one – and only one – Big Idea in every passage of Scripture, like a precious stone waiting to be dug out of the text by our efforts. As I said in the previous chapter, experience and Scripture itself tell against this, as God can and does speak through the same passage in different ways at different times in different contexts. A second danger is that we either squeeze a rich and multifaceted text into a straitjacket, or end up with a Big Idea so vague as to be meaningless. For example, what's the Big Idea in the Sermon on the Mount? Some passages clearly do not lend themselves to one-point preaching. Nonetheless, if we bear these caveats in mind, the idea of a single focus – of being able to sum up the main thrust of our sermon in a single sentence – is obviously a good discipline to get into, and there will be many occasions when a sponge cake proves just right.

The three-point sermon (the Battenberg)

In many evangelical churches, it is the three-point sermon which reigns supreme, and has done for many years. It is said that the great nineteenth-century preacher C. H. Spurgeon asked a trainee clergyman to preach an impromptu sermon on the subject of Zacchaeus. His response was a model three-pointer: "First, Zacchaeus was a man of very small stature; so am I. Second, Zacchaeus was very much up a tree; so am I. Third, Zacchaeus made haste and came down; so will I." His fellow students cheered and shouted for more, but Spurgeon reportedly said, "He could not improve upon that if he tried."

I have to come clean and confess that the three-pointer is my style on many Sundays, so why do I like it, and what are its weaknesses? The advantage is that if the sponge cake has only one flavour, the three-point Battenberg offers sponge, jam and marzipan: a wider range of flavours for a wider range of people. It's clearly structured, particularly for the preacher, but also for the listeners. After all, when I'm travelling from A to B, it's helpful to see signposts along the way telling me that I'm still on the right route and approaching my goal. Of course there are dangers: a lengthy first point can dishearten the congregation unless it is made clear at the outset that the other two are going to be a lot shorter! And the heavy-handed preacher can give the structure – the three points – too much importance: the most significant thing about a sermon is not that people can recall our three (or however many) headings, but the impact that it has on their lives.

Why three points, and not two or four? No reason at all. As I said earlier, the structure must be the servant of the sermon, not its master. For instance, if you're preaching on the names or titles of Jesus in Matthew 1:18–25, there are two: Jesus (Saviour) and Immanuel (God with us). To bring in a third (could we sneak in Son of Man, since he's referred to as Joseph's son?) would be both unnecessary and inappropriate. Having three points is principally a question of the inbuilt human preference for triplets, rather than anything to do with the doctrine of the Trinity. In traditional tales and rhymes there are often threesomes, from the Billy Goats Gruff to the butcher, the baker and the candlestick maker. We find triplets in Jesus' parables, too: the other travellers in the Good Samaritan, for instance, or the servants to whom the master distributed talents. For myself, it is the maximum number of points I can keep in my head without losing a sense of where I am going. The story is told of a conversation overheard in Oxford between two men walking down the street, in which one is saying to the other, "And ninthly, my dear fellow..." Most of us can't keep four points in our head, let alone nine! That applies to our listeners, too. I once preached a sermon on the characters in Paul's greetings at the end of Colossians, which, given that there were ten individuals, had ten points. Each of the points was short, some extremely so, but one of the congregation said to me afterwards, "When I realised how many characters you were going to talk about, my heart sank." I couldn't blame her.

It is helpful if the points are complementary, just as the flavours in a cake should be. At times there will be an overlap with the one-pointer, in that the three points might be different facets of a larger single theme. At other times the points may emerge from a passage, as in the expository sermon, which we will come to in a moment. To avoid boring predictability, the points might relate to one another in different ways:

- a progression of thought: a → b → c
- a series of premises leading to a conclusion: *if* a and b and c, *then* x
- a series of implications or applications: *if* x *then* a, and b and c
- an exploration of a number of separate but related issues, such as the titles of Jesus mentioned earlier
- a discussion of alternatives: what about a? or b? or c?
- etc.

Another way we could ring the changes, which might be particularly appropriate for certain passages or certain occasions, is to split the sermon into three units, included at different points in the service. J. John has done this very effectively at evangelistic carol services, when the audience isn't necessarily used to sitting listening to a speaker for any length of time. But there's no reason to limit it to such occasions.

The expository sermon (the fruit cake)

Another traditional evangelical approach is the verse-by-verse exposition. This takes the listener through a passage, explaining or expounding upon each verse, each phrase, or even each word. It basically offers a Bible commentary. Again, there are obvious strengths to this approach. It could be argued that this is what the Levites did in Nehemiah 8:8: "They read from the Book of the Law of God, making it clear and giving the meaning so that the people could understand what was being read" (NIV). It takes the text seriously, avoids subjective selectivity, and at its best equips the listeners with the tools to read, understand and apply the Bible in their own lives.

As with other approaches, however, there are potential pitfalls that we need to guard against. The first is that we simply retell the passage in our own words, without truly explaining or applying it. We don't truly engage with the text, but simply provide a sort of running commentary. W. E. Sangster cites a parody in his classic work, *The Craft of Sermon Construction*: "Mother Hubbard, you see, was old; there being no mention of others, we may presume she was alone; a widow – a friendless, old, solitary widow. Yet, did she despair? Did she sit down and weep, or read a novel, or wring her hands? No! *She went to the cupboard*. And here observe that she *went* to the cupboard. She did not hop, or skip, or run, or jump, or use any other peripatetic artifice; she solely and merely *went* to the cupboard... And why did she go to the cupboard? Was it to bring forth golden goblets, or glittering, precious stones, or costly apparel, or feasts, or any other attributes of wealth? *It was to get her poor dog a bone!* Not only was the widow poor, but her dog, the sole prop of her age, was poor too." Does that ring any bells?

Almost the opposite danger is that we fix on a word or phrase in the text and use it as the launch pad for a sermon which leaves the passage far behind. Sangster again gives a very apt illustration, quoting a German preacher who one Easter Day took as his text, "On the first day of the week Mary Magdalene rose early, while it was still dark" (John 20:1). He then preached a sermon on the benefits of getting up early! We may not be so extreme, but it is easy to fall into the trap of believing that we are expounding a biblical passage while we are in fact using a verse or part of a verse to ride one of our hobby horses.

I call this kind of sermon the fruit cake because in its purest form – an exposition of each verse, in context and in sequence – it offers a whole range of delights. The danger is that we offer too much variety or simply too much, and our listeners suffer spiritual indigestion! That is why so many preachers don't actually preach the pure form, but preach by paragraphs, or pick out themes, or focus on a single verse in a longer passage. There have of course been those who in the past have preached literally verse by verse, and doggedly worked their way through the Bible in this way, though their numbers have dwindled. R. T.

Kendall is a superb speaker who spent a whole year preaching through the 25 verses of Jude, but he himself notes that "there aren't many churches on either side of the Atlantic for whom this style is very desirable or acceptable." He mentions a seventeenth-century preacher, Joseph Caryl, who preached for 50 years on the book of Job. He began with a congregation of several thousand and ended up with 50!

Once again we come back to the fact that variety is the spice of life, and the best diet is a mixed menu of different structures and styles.

The narrative sermon (the Madeleine)

The final type of sermon structure is that of a straightforward narrative – the sermon as story. I've dubbed this the Madeleine after the small French cake which triggers the "remembrance of things past" in Marcel Proust's famous novel *A la Recherche du Temps Perdu*. Although this type of preaching has not been particularly common, it is enjoying a resurgence in popularity at the moment, with entire books devoted to the subject. Obviously there is good biblical precedent: much of the Old and New Testaments are in narrative form, and Jesus, in particular, taught by telling stories. Indeed, Mark 4:34 says: "He did not say anything to them without using a parable." At the same time, however, the verse goes on, "But when he was alone with his own disciples, he explained everything." That means we will generally need to follow the story with something more explanatory and/or didactic, a point we'll look at in greater depth in Chapter 8.

Having said that, there may well be occasions when we can allow the story to speak for itself. Tom Wright, arguably one of the finest contemporary preachers in the Church of England, said that one of the most powerful and moving sermons preached at Worcester College Chapel in Oxford while he was chaplain took the form of a story. Nothing more was needed – the story conveyed the message well enough without explanation. Haddon Robinson's book *Biblical Sermons* contains a couple of examples, including an excellent imaginative retelling of the book of Esther. Apart from short children's talks, I have only once used a single story to form the entire main body of a sermon. It was a testimony from *Alpha News* of someone whose life was radically changed by the Holy Spirit, which beautifully illustrated the passage on which I was preaching, Romans 8:1–14. It was well written, fast-moving and easy to listen to, and the congregation did listen intently. I then wrapped up briefly, showing how this transformation reflected Romans Chapter 8, and encouraging the listeners to believe that this could be their experience too. It worked well, though I wouldn't do it very often.

There are obvious pitfalls; one of the worst sermon openings I have ever had to sit through was a long, dull, poorly crafted story. If it had been expanded to take up the entire sermon I would have been hard put to sit right through it! Story writing is a very different discipline from that of producing other sermons, and we are not all naturally gifted at it. There are masters of the genre like Calvin Miller, who, as well as being a superb preacher, wrote the best-selling *Singer* trilogy, but such people are few and far between. But there is published material out there, and we do believe in the power of the Holy Spirit who helps us to communicate in the best way possible.

To sum up, then: give your congregation a treat by offering them a variety of cakes on the preaching plate. Not only will it whet their appetite to keep on coming back for more, but it will help to keep you from becoming stale, too.

Chapter 5

Take-off

A preacher got up to preach one Sunday with a big sack in his hand. (This is a true story.) He told the congregation, "I have in this bag the most dangerous thing in the world," put his hand into the bag and pulled out a knife. Not just a little kitchen knife, but a great big machete. He swung it round his head, chopped the air with it, and talked about the terrible things that people had done with knives and swords. Then he said, "But the most dangerous thing in the world is not a knife," and he put the knife down.

He reached into the bag again and pulled out a pistol. He pointed it at the ceiling and fired. Five hundred Baptists jumped as one in an impeccably choreographed liturgical movement. The preacher talked about the awful things that had been done with guns: the wars, the crimes, the murders, but then he said, "Guns are not the most dangerous thing in the world," and put the gun down.

Then he reached into the bag again and pulled out a cow's tongue. It was disgusting, repulsive, hideous. Just in case people hadn't realised how revolting it was, he walked among the pews and waved it in their faces. As the sensitive began to feel nauseous, the preacher, Jim Burns, said, "*This*, my brothers and sisters, is the most dangerous thing in the world. Can a fountain send forth bitter water and sweet?" And so he began a sermon on the book of James about the power of the tongue.

I don't think there's any doubt that everyone in the church was listening to Jim Burns at that moment. What's more, I don't think they could have missed his point about the destructive power of the tongue. It was a brilliant way of grabbing the congregation's attention. People who send out junk mail are told how to get a customer hooked: AIDA. Not an opera by Verdi but an acronym:

- Attention
- Interest
- Desire
- Action.

This is the sequence of responses which is necessary. The first thing we have to do is to get the listener's attention. We can't assume we already have it; we can't assume they want to hear what we have to say; we can't even assume that they want to hear what the Bible says. We need to grab their attention, attract their interest and make them desire to hear more before we can do anything about stirring them into action. As a result, just as take-off is a crucial moment in a flight, so the opening of a sermon is an equally decisive point. In this chapter we're therefore going to concentrate on the first few minutes of the message. If we can't get the sermon off the ground, we're not going to get very far! If we fail to capture people's attention right at the outset, we risk leaving them in the departure lounge.

Grabbing attention

How many sermons can you remember from over 20 years ago? A remarkable opening which I can still vividly remember was in an all-age sermon about Moses going before Pharaoh in Exodus Chapter 7. "Moses was holding his stick," the preacher said, holding up a stick, "and he threw the stick down on the ground... I won't throw this one down because it will only make a mess on the floor." She dropped the stick behind her in the pulpit and continued, "Then the stick turned into a snake!" and held up a coiled boa constrictor. The people at the back said afterwards how realistic it looked. The people at the front, like me, could see its tongue going in and out. She then matter-of-factly put the snake down behind her and continued with the sermon. Believe me, we were gripped! True, we kept checking under the pews throughout the rest of the service, but we certainly listened avidly to what the preacher had to say about Moses and Pharaoh.

A dramatic and unexpected start to the sermon can thus grab the attention and stay in the memory long after the service has ended. A curate I knew gathered the children around the crib one Christmas family service and asked them what was missing. They looked at the crib and everything seemed to be there: all the characters in the Christmas story, all the animals, everything they expected to see. "But what's missing?" he repeated. They shook their heads. They couldn't think of anything. "This is what's missing!" he said, and emptied a bucket of manure on the church floor. It was such a powerful message – Jesus came not to the hygienic surroundings of a maternity ward or even the cosy cleanliness of many stables on Christmas cards, but to the filth of a real stable. In another Christmas address I borrowed a baby from a member of the congregation who had recently given birth and dropped it on the way back to the front of church! We had switched it for a doll minutes before, but nobody had noticed. Even the children knew you mustn't drop babies! It brought the point home to people how fragile and vulnerable God became in Jesus.

Of course there is a danger that we can go over the top, like the terribly misguided sermon in Scotland in 1997, when an armed man in combat fatigues burst into the church during a scout service. He frog-marched a trussed-up church official to the front of the church, pointed a gun at the minister's head and shouted at him to come with him. Children watched in horror as the intruder blind-folded the vicar and led him out of the building. Moments later the congregation heard two shots, and some of the children were in tears when the minister reappeared and said, "See, I'm still alive!" To make matters worse, it was just three weeks before the first anniversary of the Dunblane massacre, in which 16 children and their teacher had been shot dead in a Scottish school. (As a result of the stunt, the minister and his helper were found guilty of breach of the peace by Hamilton Sheriff's court, and the minister fined £500. Four church officials also resigned in protest.)

Some might think that Jim Burns' sermon on James falls into this category, and I would agree in a British context, where gun ownership is strictly controlled. But you can still use it in your own preaching, not by imitating it but by retelling the story. It's obviously not as dramatic, but it's still pretty gripping! Incidentally, if you want some other ideas on how to go over the top, take a leaf out of the book of the minister of the Phoenix First Assembly Church in Arizona. He has flown to heaven on invisible wires, felled a tree at the front of church with a chainsaw, and included an elephant, a kangaroo and a zebra in his nativity scene (don't ask me how he brought them into the story).

Show and tell

We don't need to have drama at the front of church to capture people's attention – another form of visual aid is to use pictures, on PowerPoint, on OHP, or even just on a large piece of card if the church doesn't have high-tech capabilities. For example, I recently displayed on our OHP some of those clever pictures which show two different images, depending on which way you look at them: two faces or a goblet; a duck or a rabbit; an old woman or a young woman. (If you haven't a clue what I'm talking about, look at Alexander Sturgis's book *Magic in Art* [Belitha Press] or search for "optical illusions" on an internet image browser.) That led into a sermon about seeing things from two points of view: in that particular case how different the Christmas story looked from the perspective of Augustus and Quirinius on the one hand, or Mary and Joseph on the other. It could equally serve as an introduction to numerous passages about Jesus and the scribes of his day.

Another way of using images is to make up an "odd one out" quiz as on the TV show, *Have I Got News for You*.

One week we had Jeffrey Archer, Richard Nixon, Anthony Blunt and the apostle Peter. The congregation soon established that they were all liars, and it didn't take them long to work out that the first three had all covered up their crimes but ultimately paid the price, while Peter owned up to his sin and found forgiveness. That led us into the scene by the lakeside in John Chapter 21.

Even more simple is just showing a series of images – as long as they're clearly visible (beware of pillars!) and interesting. For instance, in a sermon on Daniel Chapter 2, I began by showing the congregation photographs of the magnificent Ishtar Gate at Babylon, which was built by Nebuchadnezzar, and restored by Saddam Hussein. The parallels between the two empire-building Iraqi dictators were striking, and it wasn't difficult to bring out the contemporary relevance of the story. On another occasion, when I was preaching on the annunciation, I showed a series of very different depictions of the scene by different artists in different centuries, and asked the congregation what *their* image of the virgin Mary was like.

Having said all that, there are potential pitfalls. One is that whatever we use to attract people's interest can draw attention to itself and stop there, rather than leading people into the sermon. I once started a sermon by showing the congregation some images of the world in which Abraham lived, including pictures of the ziggurat at Ur and Stonehenge. Someone came up to me afterwards and said, "That was very interesting." "Thank you," I murmured with appropriate humility, and she carried on, "Yes, to think that Stonehenge was already up by then – fascinating!" That duly brought me down to earth.

Words still work

Less visual, but beloved of many evangelical preachers, is to start the sermon with a story, especially a funny story. Cultured despisers and biblical purists may scorn the technique: I read in one book on preaching, "Audiences may still laugh at the joke, but they automatically discredit a speaker who treats them with so little dignity." I beg to differ. Not only is this not my experience, either as a speaker or as a listener, but opening with a story serves at least three invaluable purposes. First of all, it gets people to sit up and listen, because most people like hearing stories, especially funny ones. Secondly, it creates a rapport between the speaker and the listeners, because we're sharing something with them rather than preaching something at them. Thirdly, it raises their expectation (assuming that it's a story worth listening to) that we're going to go on sharing interesting or entertaining things with them, rather than boring or browbeating them. All of this is worth its weight in gold. And it means that the congregation will probably keep on listening to our sermon, for a while at least, which is precisely what we want. So don't be afraid of being hackneyed or clichéd by starting with a story or a joke!

There'll be a lot more about finding and using stories in Chapter 8, but I would like to make a plea that we try to find *relevant* illustrations to start the sermon: stories which have something to do with what follows. There is a tendency for some speakers simply to tell a funny story, then to give a totally unrelated message. It's true that making people laugh at the start of a sermon is beneficial for the reasons I've just outlined, but it seems to me that the opening ought then to lead on to the subject that follows, however tenuously. Otherwise, to continue our plane journey metaphor, it's as if we tell people we're flying them to Paris but then travel via Oslo. Of course, it usually takes a lot more time to find something appropriate, and in fact finding the way into a sermon is for me often the most time-consuming part of sermon preparation, but it's time well spent. Again, like take-off in an aeroplane, it's when the engines need maximum power.

But why stop at one illustration? I will often start with two or three stories on a theme, rather than just one (though that of course depends on finding that many). There can be great value in spending longer on the *entrée*, seeing it as part of the whole meal rather than just an appetiser. True, the length of our introduction is to some extent governed by the length of the sermon – if we only preach a 10- or 12-minute homily, we haven't got long for an introduction. But for the listeners, who don't know what else is coming, it sets the tone of the whole sermon. So either make it fascinating, or make it fun! Ask yourself this question: Do your congregation sit up in anticipation when you begin your sermon, or do they slump back in their seats, wondering how long this is going to last? As Haddon Robinson says, "Unfortunately the 'Great Awakening' in some churches is the moment when the sermon ends and the congregation stand for the final hymn." When Jesus spoke, I very much doubt that this was the case. Invest in the opening, because that investment will pay dividends during the rest of the sermon.

Quizzes can be another good starter, even with an

adult congregation. Use questions which don't just test whether anyone was listening to the Bible reading but reinforce people's knowledge and understanding. My problem with the game *Bible Trivia* is that trivia is just that – trivial. I have a quiz book which includes such gems as, "In describing God's control of the weather [in Psalm 147], the Psalmist does not refer to a) winds, b) clouds, c) snow or d) thunder?" The answer is thunder, if you were wondering. But does it really matter? I'm not sure I would actually set a quiz on Psalm 147, but if I had to, I suggest that more helpful questions would be along the lines of: "What does God do for the brokenhearted?" (A: heals them and binds up their wounds: verse 3) or "According to the Psalmist, to how many nations did God reveal his law?" (A: one, Israel: "He has revealed his word to Jacob, his laws and decrees to Israel. He has done this for no other nation": verses 19–20). I would, however, only use this latter question in an adult talk, because children (and, I suspect, many adults!) could not be expected to know that Jacob and Israel are one and the same. So there's a subsidiary teaching point, alongside the issue of revelation of the law, and, if you're really keen, and you think it would benefit the congregation, you could even throw in something about Hebrew parallelism at the same time. What I would strongly emphasise, however, is that it is very important that we don't make anybody look stupid! That demotivates the congregation and creates a barrier between us and them, the very opposite of what we are trying to achieve.

By this point in the chapter some readers may be beginning to feel a little unhappy. Isn't the line I'm proposing selling out to our culture, pandering to a generation that demands entertainment? I don't think so, because Jesus can be accused of precisely the same thing. He appears to have used a variety of different devices to attract his audience's attention and awaken their interest. One was to point to objects in the world around him: "Look at the birds of the air; they do not sow or reap or store away in barns ... " (Matthew 6:26). On another occasion he quoted a recent news story: "You know those eighteen people who died when the tower in Siloam fell on them?" (Luke 13:4). Yet another time he told a vivid story to make them sit up and listen: "A man was travelling from Jerusalem to Jericho when he was beaten up by a gang of thieves... " If this kind of opening was good enough for Jesus, it's certainly good enough for me!

What about the Bible?

Another concern in the minds of some readers may be that I haven't mentioned beginning with the Bible, and you're wondering why. The reason is simple: for a contemporary congregation, I believe that there is such a gulf between the biblical world and our own, we have to start where we are before we go back into the Bible. What is more, we can no longer assume either that our listeners are familiar with the Bible, or that they approach a sermon wanting to be taught about the Bible. I would expect some argument over that – some of you may say that in your congregation there certainly *is* that expectation. But are we really only preaching to our established congregations? Or isn't our hope and our heart's desire that we will regularly see newcomers joining our numbers, whether they are friends of church members, graduates from the *Alpha* course, or simply interested outsiders? If the church's decline is not to continue, and if indeed it is going to be reversed, we have to preach with the unchurched in mind, not only at guest services and the major festivals, but all the time. And that means starting where people are at, which is not with the Bible.

Let me quote some statistics about one of the best-known bits of the Bible, the Christmas story, to prove my point. An ON-Digital survey found that although two-thirds of adults knew why Mary and Joseph had gone to Bethlehem, among 18–24-year-olds that figure dropped to one-fifth (yes, just 20%!). The same proportion of 18–24-year-olds could name Herod as the king involved in the Christmas story, and less than half of all adults questioned could do so. Even the most familiar stories, which we often assume "everyone knows", are no longer familiar in twenty-first-century Britain. To attract the attention and maintain the interest of the modern unchurched generation we have to start where they're at, which means we can't start with the Bible.

Having said that, I trust that the examples I have given show how our aim is to draw people into the biblical world. To use John Stott's image, we build a bridge from the modern world into the world of the Bible. What we want to do in our opening is to make that crossing as easy as possible, so that people immediately begin to see the relevance of the Bible passage we are studying together.

If we're going to preach with the unchurched in mind, we must also remember that they are not used to sitting through sermons. Just as captain and cabin crew seek to comfort nervous airline passengers before take-off, so we too might like to help them relax before the flight. I'm not suggesting we start the sermon by indicating the emergency exits, but rather by giving them some idea of where we're going, and perhaps some idea of how long it might take. Different sermons will have different approaches, but somewhere near the start of the sermon, after an opening illustration or two, we might say something like: "In the next 20 minutes we'll look at how God speaks to us today – and how we can learn to hear his voice." Or: "This passage from the Bible tackles a question which is so relevant, namely, how are we to react when suffering comes?" Or: "Paul gives us five principles for giving that still apply to us," and then list them.

To sum up: we need to work hard on the start of the sermon, because it's a critical moment, perhaps the *most* critical. We really don't want to crash and burn on the runway! A good opening will therefore:

- capture people's attention
- relate to what follows
- draw people into the Bible.

and one characteristic that I haven't mentioned, but which will I trust commend itself without further explanation:

- vary from week to week.

Chapter 6   Coming in to land

It is said that the great fourth-century preacher John Chrysostom ("Golden-mouth") used to be applauded at the end of his sermons. That may be too much to ask, but how can we ensure that we bring the sermon smoothly in to land?

Sometimes the problem is that the preacher has prepared too much and suddenly realises that his time is up – rather like the aircraft that's running out of fuel. He has to get down somehow, and, looking at the congregation fidgeting and muttering, as quickly as possible. So he shuffles a few pages of notes, misses out the next two points (or six verses) and rapidly comes to the conclusion. The trouble is that what the congregation receives is not the sermon that was prepared. The structure's been blown out of the water and the result may be totally unbalanced. Picking up the biblical image of food being laid on the table, it's like taking away the main course before the customer's finished eating it, telling them there's no time for dessert or coffee, and bringing the bill. Nobody would leave a tip after that kind of service!

At other times it's the opposite difficulty – the preacher doesn't quite know how to land. He circles the airstrip, looking for the right point to touch down.

Evangelists are especially prone to this: "In a minute I'm going to pray a prayer..." Then they take you through the prayer. In detail. "I want you to pray this prayer with me if you mean it, blah, blah... but some of you may not be ready, in which case, blah, blah... and some of you may have prayed it many times before, blah, blah..." Then a new topic: "And I'll be standing at the door with a booklet, which tells you blah, blah... and, if you pray that prayer, I want you to tell someone, blah, blah..." By this time some who were thinking of praying the prayer have forgotten why they were going to! But, if I'm honest, I know I've done it too, not in evangelistic appeals but in ordinary sermons, looking for just the right phrase to finish on, not quite satisfied with *that* one, so coming round again to find another, and another... Best at that point just to cut my losses and land, even if it's a bit bumpy, or we could all be up there all night. As Calvin Miller says, "A surgeon will stop her surgery when she knows her patient has died on the operating table... A cowboy will dismount when he knows for sure his horse is dead. Only preachers keep on preaching after they've run out of sermon."

Preparation is obviously crucial. If I have prepared the sermon properly, I won't run out of time. I actually practise my sermon with a stopwatch – I walk round the study and preach it to my bookshelves and then see at the end (without peeking beforehand) how long I've taken. That shows me if I've got room for a little more or, more often, if there's a need for pruning. (I put net curtains on the study windows after a member of the congregation saw me pacing round the study practising my sermon and wondered what on earth I was doing!) At the same time I know that, in delivery, the sermon will almost certainly take longer than in rehearsal, because I'll probably repeat myself a bit, I'll pause more often, and I may speak more slowly. Given my style of preaching, which is discussed in the next chapter, I may also go off in other directions – though this is compensated for by the fact that I may miss out bits. But the general rule of thumb is that the sermon in church is likely to be a few minutes longer than the one in the study.

As for finding just the right ending, the problem can be that we spend so long getting the beginning just right and then working on the main body of the sermon that there isn't a lot of time left to spend on the ending. And, frankly, by the time we are writing it up we just want to get it over and done with, not rework the ending as many times as we've already reworked the beginning. A little more time in the study would save a lot of grief in the pulpit. Even if we don't write the whole sermon out word for word, this is one part that might benefit from that. And rather than just write down the first thing that comes into our head, we need to work and rework the ending until we're happy with it. Because, as we shall consider in a moment, our conclusion, the last thing that people hear, can have a powerful impact. As Stuart Briscoe says, we don't want to be like the Israelites at Jericho, going round and round and then the whole thing falls flat!

Landing back in the real world

Timing and wording are not the only things we need to bear in mind when working on the close of our sermon. I believe that the conclusion of the sermon must also involve application. Having started where our listeners are and taken them back into the world of the Bible, we mustn't leave them there as if, like the characters in some Hollywood film, the time machine has broken down and they're stranded in ancient Israel. We need to bring them back into the everyday world of today and show how what we've just seen in Scripture makes a difference to our lives in the twenty-first century. The curate at a church I used to attend would sometimes be brought down to earth by his wife after his profound biblical expositions by the question, "Yes, but what use is that to me on Monday morning?"

The big question at the end of every sermon therefore needs to be: "So what?" Because that is what many of the congregation will be asking themselves, either subconsciously or – like my curate's wife – out loud. We need to show how the Bible relates to contemporary life. Spurgeon once said of a type of preacher, "He is great upon the ten toes of the beast, the four faces of the cherubim, the mystical meaning of badgers' skins, and the typical bearings of the staves of the ark and the windows of Solomon's temple; but the sins of the businessman, the temptations of the times and the needs of the age, he scarcely ever touches upon." I myself have come across preachers who think that all we need to do is expound the Scriptures and leave the Holy Spirit to make the application. I believe this approach is fundamentally flawed: it is our job not just to expound, but also to apply.

Let me illustrate. In the Old West, the minister of a frontier town was walking by the river one day when he saw members of his congregation down by the water's edge, dragging some logs ashore. He could see that each log had the owner's name stamped on the end, and he was horrified to see his church members bringing out their saws and cutting off the end with the tell-tale mark. He resolved that he could not let the matter pass. So the following Sunday he preached a powerful sermon on the commandment, "Thou shalt not steal." But to his dismay, one after another of the people he'd seen down by the river shook him by the hand as they left the church, saying things like, "Mighty fine sermon, pastor," or, "That was a wonderful message." The pastor spent the week pondering his next move, and in the end decided on his plan of action. The following Sunday he preached exactly the same sermon as the previous week, word for word, until the very end. As he summed up, instead of saying, "And so, my friends, the Bible is clear: Thou shalt not steal," as he had the previous week, he said: "And so, my friends, the Bible is clear: Thou shalt not cut the end off thy neighbour's logs." They ran him out of town!

If you still need convincing, look at the Bible itself, where the sermons of the New Testament offer prime examples. For instance, in the synagogue in Nazareth, Jesus took an Old Testament text, Isaiah Chapter 61, and made the application: "Today this scripture is fulfilled in your hearing" (Luke 4:21). In Acts Chapter 7, Stephen expounded a string of Old Testament texts and declared, even more bluntly than that preacher in the Old West, "You stiff-necked people, with uncircumcised hearts and ears! You are just like your fathers: You always resist the Holy Spirit!" (7:51). In the Epistles, too, theological discussion leads to application. In Romans 12:1, for example, a lengthy exposition on the Jews' place in God's plan of salvation is followed by the words, "I urge you, *therefore ...*" and instructions on how to live. As Haddon Robinson says: "Application is not incidental to effective expository preaching, it is crucial."

This of course raises the question: *How* do we go about applying the message? Here we really do need inspiration from the Holy Spirit. We can perspire over the text and read countless commentaries, but they won't give us an application for our congregation. Of course, some types of commentaries do offer application. One series is actually entitled the *NIV Application Commentary* and includes a "Contemporary Significance" section after each passage, as well as an "Original Meaning" section and one called "Bridging Contexts". Yet the usefulness of this is limited by the fact that it has to be a very general application and will not necessarily have any relevance for our particular people. We need to preach to their world and their situations in the light of our shared experience. I'll discuss this at greater length in the chapter on using illustrations (see Chapter 8), but in a nutshell, our applications must be appropriate. For example, if we're preaching on guidance, it's not particularly helpful to use as an application the issue of finding the right marriage partner in a church with no eligible adults. One approach which I have found useful is to think of three or four different people in the congregation who are representative of the whole and then to ask myself, "What would this message mean to them?" This encourages a variety of applications. So, for example, preaching recently on finding a time and place to pray each day, I didn't simply suggest that we should all copy Jesus by getting up very early and finding a solitary place (cf. Mark 1:35). Some people's situations may permit this, but for many people it's just not feasible. I suggested we could pray while out walking the dog, driving the car, going to work, in the lunch hour, or even in the bath. A trivial example, I know, but illustrative of the need to think ourselves into different people's situations with imagination – and inspiration.

Making an impact

This brings me to another important aspect of the close of a sermon – its purpose. If the beginning of a sermon is crucial because it determines whether people will listen to us or not, the ending is equally critical because it affects what they will do with what they have heard. To go back to AIDA, it determines whether the sermon will lead to action. Adlai Stevenson said, "When Socrates spoke, the people said, 'How inspiring,' but when Demosthenes spoke, the people said, 'Let us march!'" That's surely the impact we want to have: not just to share information, but to change lives. So the preacher has to ask him- or herself the question: "What do I want this sermon to do?", not "What do I want this sermon to say?" Or, better still, "What does *God* want to do through this sermon?" As I said in the previous chapter, I do not think that the mark of a good sermon is whether the congregation remember that I preached on Providence, Perseverance and Passion (or whatever). Far more significant are questions such as: Do they have a greater trust in God's providence, a stronger desire to persevere or a deeper passion for Jesus? And in that situation, two out of three really ain't bad!

Nehemiah Chapter 8 provides a wonderful illustration of this. The Levites read from the Book of the Law, "making it clear and giving the meaning so that the people could understand what was being read" (verse 8). As a result, the people started weeping as the preaching of God's word convicted them. But then Nehemiah and the Levites said, "Go and enjoy choice food and sweet drinks, and send some to those who have nothing prepared. This day is sacred to our Lord. Do not grieve, for the joy of the Lord is your strength" (verse 10). And the passage goes on: "Then all the people went away to eat and drink, to send portions of food and to celebrate with great joy, because they now understood the words that had been made known to them." The preacher helped them to understand what they had heard – feeding their *minds* – but then also brought them encouragement and joy, touching their *emotions*. This is our goal: to preach to the whole person: mind, heart and will.

Of course the difficulty is that to a certain extent the impact of the sermon is beyond our control. We can preach our heart out, deliver the finest sermon we have ever preached, and yet still it falls on deaf ears. Will Willimon tells how a fellow preacher in the USA once did a survey to measure the congregation's racial attitudes, preached a series of five sermons about racial tolerance, and then issued the survey again. He found that they were now three per cent more racist than before! In the synagogue at Nazareth Jesus preached a powerful sermon, called for a response, and faced rejection. This was the apostles' repeated experience as well. It is our job to preach, and the Holy Spirit's to convict. Even so, I believe that there is an obligation for us to plan to preach for a response. As in the story of the logs I quoted earlier, it may not always be the response we are hoping for, but then it has always been the preacher's job to afflict the comfortable as well as to comfort the afflicted. We need to prepare, to preach, and, if necessary, to provoke. As François de Sales said, "The test of a preacher is that his congregation goes away saying not, 'What a lovely sermon,' but, 'I will do something!'" We need to make sure that in our preparation and our delivery we know what we want the sermon to do, and what we want our congregation to do in response. That's our responsibility. It's up to the listeners and the Holy Spirit to do the rest.

Ten feet above contradiction?

One area of preaching which we have not considered so far is the whole question of dialogue and feedback, and one little-used but often very profitable way of ending a sermon is to offer an opportunity to ask questions. I suggest that this is preferable to taking questions on the hoof in the course of a sermon. I have had people interrupt my preaching with a question which I've attempted to answer, but if this keeps happening, it tends to be disruptive for the listeners as well as the preacher. It can be hard to maintain the thread of an argument if there are regular interruptions, particularly if they are going off in all directions.

Opening up for questions at the end is very different,

and can be highly profitable. It ensures that there is opportunity for disagreement and genuine dialogue, gives room for clarification, and allows the congregation to explore specific areas more deeply. Two obvious reservations spring to mind: on the one hand, there might not be sufficient time to preach a sermon of a decent length and allow space for discussion, and, on the other, we may not feel able to answer all the questions. It is said that Gregory of Nazianzus was once asked a question to which he replied, "I would rather answer that one in the pulpit!" The question of time is one which has to be determined locally. Due warning can be given, so that most people come expecting a longer service. Could other elements of the service be cut, to allow more time? Is there a time of day which is better than the principal service? An evening often offers greater opportunity, as the dinner isn't in the oven. As for the second concern, that we may not know all the answers, I don't see this as an obstacle at all. It is good for our congregation to see that we don't think we have all the answers and to hear an honest, "I don't know" from time to time. It can also open up a real discussion among those present rather than just a dialogue between preacher and congregation.

I have included an opportunity for questions on different occasions. I think it can be particularly helpful in the context of sermons that we expect to be controversial (see Chapter 10, "Handling hot potatoes"). For instance, after a sermon in which I argued from Daniel Chapter 2 that I did not believe that it was right for the United Kingdom to go to war with Iraq, I wanted to give people who had a different viewpoint the chance to express their views. In fact, to my surprise (and relief), nobody disagreed, and I had more positive feedback on that sermon than on many others. Other contexts in which time for discussion can be especially useful is after sermons which are complex – say, on the book of Revelation – or of particular pastoral concern. To give another example from my own experience, a colleague and I answered questions after a sermon on life after death, which was greatly appreciated. Don't worry if nobody has any questions. Stuart Briscoe, who is a very gifted speaker, once delivered a whole week of sermons at a church in South Carolina. At the end of the week there was a question-and-answer session. After a long silence, an elderly lady in the front row asked, "Is them your own teeth?"

Of course, it is possible to use dialogue throughout a sermon, breaking for discussion at regular intervals. I know of one church that has made this the regular format of its alternative morning service, and this has proved so popular that they now find it hard to fit everyone in. In my former church we used this kind of format on summer evenings in place of home groups, and this annual "Summer school" gave us the opportunity to tackle issues of a nature and in a manner that wouldn't be possible in a normal service. The idea was to include worship and teaching, but also to offer the chance for questions and/or discussion. We looked at controversial topics such as a Christian view of Europe, homosexuality, and remarriage after divorce, and broad themes that wouldn't normally be covered in a sermon, like Celtic spirituality, insights from biblical archaeology, or an overview of the Old Testament. As you might imagine, preparing these evenings took a lot longer than preparing a regular sermon. But it proved extremely worthwhile.

Review

The service is over, the sermon has been preached, and most of us probably want to forget about it and move on. But there is one more thing we can do which can prove extremely helpful, and that is the process of review, either by ourselves or by others.

Obviously there may well be comments at the door. I have an old Punch cartoon in which a man is coming out of church doing up his coat and saying to his wife, "An indifferent sermon, but an amusing little wine." The trouble is that such comments are often (usually?) unrepresentative – my experience is that I can preach a really challenging message and get the response, "Lovely sermon," which is not quite the response I was aiming for! And we all know that some people are so polite that they will thank us to our face and then tear the sermon to bits on the way home, while the vast majority will say nothing at all, whether they profoundly disagree or feel deeply moved.

So we need to do something more systematic. The first step is our own self-review. The Sunday before last I realised, on the way home after the service, that the sermon hadn't really ended where it had begun, but had somehow gone off on another tack during the final revision. It wasn't heretical (at least I don't think it was), but it certainly could have been better. And sometimes we will end up asking ourselves whether we haven't in fact misinterpreted the passage. Stuart Briscoe writes: "People still remind me about a message I gave on John Mark and Barnabas. I preached that John Mark was frightened. In fact I called him 'Chicken John Mark'. Then I started thinking about that allegation. *Although Scripture says he left Paul and Barnabas in the middle of their journey, it doesn't say why. Maybe I'm giving John Mark a bum rap. I'll be spending eternity with him, and I don't want him coming up to me saying, 'Hey Buddy, who are you calling chicken?'"*

The other step we can take is to ask for feedback on a particular sermon, or indeed on all our preaching. The person who has taught me most about this subject is Bill Hybels. In an article originally published in *Leadership Journal* and reproduced in *Mastering Contemporary Preaching*, this highly gifted communicator reveals the level of feedback to which he regularly submits himself. I put it like that because I have to admit that I don't find it easy. My preacher's ego is a delicate, fragile thing, which can shatter at the slightest hint of criticism. We don't want other people telling us the flaws in our preaching; we want them flattering us! To quote Garrison Keillor in *Lake Wobegon Days*: "Under this thin veneer of modesty lies a monster of greed. I drive away faint praise, beating my little chest, waiting to be named Sun-God, King of America, Idol of Millions, Bringer of Fire, The Great Haji, Thun-Dar The Boy Giant. I don't want to say, 'Thanks, glad you liked it.' I want to say, 'Rise my people. Remove your faces from the carpet, stand, look me in the face.'"

But back to Bill Hybels. He is in the unusual position of preaching the same sermon three times: once on Saturday night and then twice on Sunday morning. So getting immediate feedback has immediate relevance, as the message can then be fine-tuned and anything unfortunate or unhelpful filtered out. Most of us are not in that situation, although some larger churches do have a repeated morning service where this could be directly applicable. Bill Hybels has his elders evaluate his message as he preaches it, and give him their comments within minutes of the end of the service. One elder, whom he trusts as the most discerning, collects the other elders' responses, summarises them (so that he doesn't read the same criticism three times over!), and gives that summary to the preacher before he leaves. It's then up to him how much notice to take of the comments, though the elders are obviously people whose opinions he respects, and they know, too, the need to be sensitive when criticising their pastor.

We may or may not have an eldership team, but the same principles apply. If we want useful reactions to the sermon, we need to have it from the right people at the right time and in the right way. The *right people* are those whom we know to be supportive of our ministry and yet confident enough to speak the truth (in love!), and whose judgment we respect. Imagine you're making a hospital visit and the patient says to you: "You are the most amazing preacher I have ever heard. Your messages are anointed from God! Every time I hear you speak it's as if God himself speaks to my heart." The nature of your response will depend on whether you're visiting a member of your congregation in a surgical ward or a patient in a psychiatric ward who has just told you that he's Jesus Christ. At the *right time* means that those who critique us must be able to take notes during the sermon and to respond promptly. Because I don't repeat my talks, straight after the service, when there are other people to see and other issues to tackle, would not be the best time. But some time before the following sermon is essential. As for the *right way* in which people comment, I have found it helpful to give some guidance as to what they should be looking for. This has the added advantage of balancing any negatives there may be with some positive areas, since the aim of the whole exercise is to encourage and improve, not to demolish and demoralise. I have consequently produced an A4 checklist with the following headings and room for notes:

Practicalities
- Volume/clarity
- Speed of delivery
- Mannerisms
- Use of notes/eye contact
- Body language

Generalities
- What do you think was the aim of the sermon?
- How easy was it to follow the development of the sermon?
- How was the Bible used?
- What illustrations were used, and how appropriate/helpful were they?
- How suitable was the sermon for this congregation?
- How relevant was it to Monday morning?
- What did you get out of it?

One final thought on this topic. In the aforementioned article, Bill Hybels explained that one of his reasons for adopting this approach was the very unrepresentative nature of the comments he received at the door or during the week by letter or phone call. The people who would wait to speak to him or go to the bother of contacting him were often needy and dysfunctional people, people desperate for help. So when he preached on "God will be with you even in your pain," the feedback was tremendous and overwhelmingly positive. Challenging messages about lifestyle were less well received, so he subconsciously began to preach more and more "therapy", less and less "discipleship". It was once he realised what he was doing that he instituted this formalised method of getting feedback, as well as a longer-term pattern of sermon planning. Though I don't get 100 to 150 people contacting me about my sermons every week as Bill Hybels does, I recognise the truth of his observation in my own situation. Systematic review can be a very useful tool in improving our preaching.

Chapter 7   Style

In his book *The Empowered Communicator*, Calvin Miller says, "They arrested a man the other day. They threw him in jail. He was walking around town in a white robe carrying a sign that said, 'THE WORLD IS COMING TO AN END'. I don't know why they arrested him. As I saw it, he was telling the truth interestingly. Last week my preacher preached on that very thing. The way he told that same truth wasn't all that interesting. They might have locked up the wrong man."

How interesting are we in the pulpit? How can we make ourselves more interesting? In this chapter I want to look at the kind of script we use, the kind of voice we adopt and even where we stand, and how these things can help or hinder the task of communication. My prayer at the start of every Sunday service is that I won't get in the way of God speaking to these people, either by the words I use or by the way I use them. I want these people to encounter God and hear him speak to them, and I'll do anything I can to minimise the risk of me being a blockage rather than a blessing.

Climbing out of the pulpit

There's an apocryphal story of a minister who had a church building project and asked the elders if he could keep one detail of the plans secret. They agreed, as long as they could have their secret too. When it came to the day of the grand opening, the minister stood up in the pulpit at the start of the service and pressed a red button. Immediately the empty front pew disappeared into the ground and the second pew moved to the front. And the back row barrackers saw another pew rise out of the ground behind them. As the service went on, the minister found himself wondering what the elders' secret was. It wasn't until he was ten minutes into his 45-minute sermon that he discovered. An elder pressed a button, a trapdoor in the pulpit opened up, and the organist started playing the final hymn.

Where do you preach from? If it's a pulpit, may I ask why? In a few – I suggest a very few – church buildings the only place where the preacher is visible is actually "high and lifted up", so there's really no choice. In the vast majority of churches, however, we would communicate much better if we moved down from our lofty perch, out from behind the barrier, and actually talked to people face to face. We don't want to sacrifice visibility and audibility, but the closer we are to the congregation, and the nearer to their level, the better. The same applies to standing behind a lectern. It's a barrier which creates distance between speaker and listeners. If we can possibly find a way of holding our notes without that dividing wall between us, it's well worth the effort. There are, of course, practical difficulties. In many Anglican churches, pillars are one! But they are an obstacle wherever we preach from, even a pulpit. Unless the church is so full that there's standing room only – not a problem that most of us face – people can actually move a little so that they can see you. If they want to, of course. Because we need to acknowledge that some people will be deeply uncomfortable with the preacher coming nearer to them. They prefer him/her to be safely remote so that they can be undisturbed and unchallenged. Needless to say, this is not a good reason for maintaining the status quo!

Another practical problem may be amplification. Yet it ceases to be a problem if we invest in a radio microphone, which is not going to blow a hole in most church budgets. In saying this I am assuming that every church should have a microphone for the preacher and an effective sound system. Unfortunately there are still a few speakers who like to think that they don't need to use a microphone because they have a powerful voice. The problem is that, however loudly they speak, it is unlikely that those who suffer from impaired hearing will be able to hear unless they're using a microphone linked to a loop system. And since we want our churches to be places where the disabled can take a full part in worship, we need to include rather than exclude the hard of hearing. There is another benefit for preachers, too, namely that with a microphone we don't need to raise our voices all the time. Even though we still need to project our voice, we can vary the pitch and tone, even whisper, and thereby improve our communication skills still further.

Dropping our notes

When I began preaching, I wrote a full script. It was my father, an experienced preacher, who told me to write on just one side of the paper so as to avoid that awkward pause when you have to turn a page. The first sermon I ever preached (of which I'm sure I would be deeply ashamed if I looked at it now) was simply read out. Certainly I remember gripping the pulpit tightly throughout most of the time I was up there! Now I would say to any and every preacher, teacher, lecturer and speaker: *please don't read your script!* There is little that more effectively sabotages meaningful communication than the sound of a voice reading from a script, particularly since the need to keep eyes down on the written or printed page prevents eye contact with the listeners.

If this makes you want to throw down the book in alarm and cry, "But I can't do anything else!", let me say that there is a way of preaching with a full script that does not involve straight eyes-down reading. My father modelled the technique, I managed to pick it up, and I know many colleagues in ministry who communicate successfully from a full script. The skill lies in knowing the material so well – after all, you meditated upon it, wrote it, rewrote it, indeed, gave birth to it! – that you look down at the script, your eye picks out a sentence or a phrase at a time, you look up and deliver it, and then glance back down again to see what comes next. Of course, if the sermon is properly constructed, you've a good idea where you're going next even before you look. It is thus perfectly possible to "read" an entire sermon without sounding as if you're reading at all. Because it is the *sound* of the reader, that subtle change in tone which is instantly detectable to the listener, that kills interest.

If you can manage to preach without reading your script verbatim, why not move on another stage and preach from notes or headings? The benefit of this is that every sentence that comes out is genuinely natural speech, not a literary construct. Because the great weakness of every scripted sermon is that it is a written text rather than an oral text, and it is well documented that people speak differently from how they write. A written style is more formal (for example, "do not" rather than "don't"), more abstract and more mannered. Let me quote, by way of example, a line from a sermon which I read recently, which the author (who will understandably remain nameless) was actually citing as an instance of good practice:

> Is it different? Knowing that the light, which was for Sarai and Abram a frequently-extinguished glint, has come – and shines out from those who are willing to go to him outside the camp, and bear the abuse he endured?

Apart from the fact that this whole second sentence is too long, I don't know of anyone who in normal everyday speech would use a phrase such as "a frequently-extinguished glint", nor who would leave such a long gap between the subject, "the light", and the verb, "has come". This kind of literary speech is a stumbling block to effective communication, and it stems from the fact that it originated in a study rather than before an audience. I am trying to write this book in an informal, chatty style, but I know that a written style keeps creeping in. It's very hard to avoid, because I'm writing!

Two preachers in particular helped me cut loose from my script. The first was a visiting speaker at the church where I was curate, who was over halfway through his sermon when I noticed his notes slip off the lectern and flutter to the ground. He did not hesitate or stumble, but smoothly carried on to the end of the talk. I remember thinking to myself, "I wish I could know my sermons so well that if that ever happened to me, I could do the same!" The other was J. John, a supremely gifted preacher and evangelist, whom I heard speak on preaching at a conference. He was funny, he was thought-provoking, he was persuasive, and he wasn't using notes. And what I took away from that afternoon was his characteristic message to "Chill out!" To put it in my words rather than his: don't worry about having everything nailed down beforehand, but know where you're going and take the people with you. That's now my approach to preaching, and I would humbly and heartily recommend it to anyone. Let me explain the process.

In the study beforehand I do all the usual preparation, work out the message, the structure, the beginning and the end, and write out a rough draft. If you were to stop me in the street at this stage in my sermon preparation, away from the study, I would be able to give you the drift of what I was going to say. Not the details, perhaps, but certainly the broad outline. Then I rehearse the sermon aloud, timing it for length, but referring to my notes as little as possible. The only things I really do need to read are the Bible and any quotes or illustrations I'm using (see the next chapter for more on those). Sometimes new insights emerge at this point, or key phrases and new illustrations come to mind. When I look back at my first draft I usually notice that some things have been missed out. That's a good time to ask myself whether they should be in the sermon at all. After all, if they haven't stuck in my mind, will they stick in anyone else's? Some are therefore dropped; others now stick more firmly in my mind because I've reconsidered them and decided they are important. Because I generally preach for 20 minutes (I'm not saying this is good or bad, it's simply the norm in my church), rehearsal and review take only about half an hour, which I trust you agree is not long at all. So ideally I go away and do something else, then repeat the process. By this stage I'm becoming really familiar with my material, and I've got the length about right. Now I write out a series of notes on a single sheet of Filofax paper (a piece of card will do just as well) which can be slipped in my Bible to act as a safety net, parachute, or whatever other metaphor you choose. So that it's fresh in my mind, this final phase needs to be not long before the sermon – for me, usually Saturday afternoon or evening for Sunday morning, and Sunday afternoon for Sunday evening. Then, when I stand up to preach, I don't have to read my notes or even refer to them most of the time, because what I want to say is clear in my mind.

Please let me emphasise: this is *not* learning the sermon off by heart and delivering it as an actor delivers lines. Each time I rehearse, and then when I actually preach, the talk is slightly (or even significantly) different.

The words I use as I preach will be fresh and new, and this will be spontaneous communication, a real conversation with the people sitting in front of me. Sure, some of my words will probably be identical to ones I used in the study, particularly any key phrases that I've latched on to (for example, while preaching on the church as the temple of the Holy Spirit last Sunday, I deliberately used the phrase, "the place where heaven and earth meet" as a *leit-motif* running through the sermon). Much of what I say will echo what I said in rehearsal; parts of it will be entirely new. But the structure will be the same and the message will be the same. And I will trust the Holy Spirit that anything really important that he wants me to say will be recalled and that anything I forget or overlook either doesn't matter or will end up in another sermon at another time. As J. John said, "Chill out!"

Look who's talking

I love the cartoon by Simon Jenkins that shows a clergy-man reading the book *Choosing a Preaching Voice*, which has a picture of Donald Duck on the cover. I don't know whether it's the fault of theological colleges, certain famous preachers who have become role models or some deep quirk of the subconscious mind, but all too many clergy have a terrible parsonical drawl just like that adopted by Alan Bennett in his wonderful parody of a sermon in the early 1960s ("Esau my brother is a hairy man, and I am a smooth man"). Calvin Miller gives some excellent advice: "It is easy to tell if you've shifted into a preacher's tone. Just listen to how long it takes you to say

God. If you find yourself stretching it into two syllables, it is time to get the phony out of your phonetics." My wife is extremely swift to nip my "vicar voice" in the bud. I've noticed that it is especially prone to come out at weddings and funerals, when the words of the liturgy are both solemn and familiar, and when my wife isn't usually present! If you haven't got an obligingly critical spouse, I urge you to ask an honest and true friend in the congregation to grimace at you if ever you start sounding like a stereotypical cleric.

Leaving aside the sort of clergyman epitomised by Derek Nimmo or Dick Emery (for those of you old enough to remember them), actors do have something to teach us about using our voice and our bodies to communicate. I have already mentioned the opportunity offered by a microphone to vary our volume, but I wonder how many of us consciously try to use a variety of pitch and tone. I don't mean as in the old joke about the comment written in the margin of some sermon notes, "Argument weak, shout louder." Rather, I'm talking about raising and lowering our voice in a natural way as we would if we were discussing these issues in a different context, say, the pub. I mean watching the speed of our delivery. I tend to talk too fast, and although the producer of the highly successful TV series *The West Wing* has apparently told his actors to speak faster because it makes them look more intelligent, that's not what my congregation say about me! We shouldn't be afraid of pausing for emphasis, stopping for a moment or two after a particular point to allow people to think about what we've just said. (This can also be a good way of waking someone whose eyelids are drooping –

they think it's all over!) Body language is important, too. We all know how Italians communicate with their whole bodies, and there's something to be said for allowing our hands to join our voices as we preach. I found that this didn't come naturally to me as a typical Englishman – I needed to make a deliberate effort to use appropriate gestures to reinforce the message of the sermon.

It isn't just our voices and our bodies which can help or hamper communication, but our vocabulary too. Martin Luther said, "I don't think of Dr Pomeranium, Jonas or Philip [Melanchthon] in my sermon. They know more about it than I do. So I don't preach to them. I just preach to Hansie or Betsy." In order to communicate with our congregations, we need to make sure that we are using language they understand. "Eschatology" and "apocalyptic" are probably not words that ever passed our lips before we started our theological training, so why should they feature in sermons? If we're using them to impress people, shame on us. If the concepts they convey are important for understanding our text, then let's work a little harder in the study to put them into words that everybody can understand. Let's not give in to sesquipedalianism, that is, using long words where short ones will do!

Let's also watch the way we speak. My German course at university primarily consisted of studying literary texts, most of them from the nineteenth century. As a result, when I visited a friend in Germany she laughed at the way I talked: grammatically correct, but formal and stilted. "Nobody talks like that!" she said. But when we went to church on Sunday, I pointed out that she was wrong: the pastor in the pulpit spoke just like me! We need to ensure that our speech doesn't get in the way of the message we're proclaiming. Having said that, this doesn't mean that we always have to be conversational, still less prosaic, for there is clearly also room for rhetoric. African-American preachers are masters at this: just think of Martin Luther King's famous "I have a dream" speech. Here's an extract from a fine example of the genre, the celebrated prayer of Pentecostal preacher Dr S. M. Lockeridge – you can find the full text on the internet (at www.jesus.org.uk/dawn/1997/dawn9701.html) or in *A Box of Delights*, by J. John and Mark Stibbe, pp. 96–97.

> The Bible says He's a seven way king.
> He's the King of the Jews – that's a racial king.
> He's the King of Israel – that's a national king.
> He's the King of righteousness.
> He's the King of the ages.
> He's the King of Heaven.
> He's the King of glory.
> He's the King of kings and He is the Lord of lords.
> Now that's my King.
> Well I wonder if you know Him?
>
> David said, "The Heavens declare the glory of God, and the firmament sheweth His handiwork." My King is a sovereign king – no means of measure can define His limitless love. No far-seeing telescope can bring into visibility the coastline of His shoreless supplies. No barrier can hinder Him from pouring out His blessing.

He's enduringly strong.
He's entirely sincere.
He's eternally steadfast.
He's immortally graceful.
He's imperially powerful.
He's impartially merciful.
Do you know him?

A clear message put across with powerful rhetoric; not my style, but undeniably great preaching!

Yet having said that there is a place for rhetoric, let me end this chapter with a warning against getting carried away and going all theatrical. With a captive audience in front of us, the pulpit becomes a stage upon which we can release all that hitherto untapped dramatic potential within us. Here's another sermon I've come across, which to my astonishment was held up as a model of "contemporary idiom". It's about Jezebel's plot to get rid of Naboth in 1 Kings 21.

Hear her derisive laugh as it rings out in the palace like the shrill cackle of a wild owl that has returned to its nest and has found a serpent therein! With her tongue, sharp as a razor, she prods Ahab as an ox driver prods with sharp goad the ox which does not want to press his neck into the yoke, or as one whips with a rawhide a stubborn mule. With profuse and harsh laughter this old gay gaudy guinea of Satan derided this king of hers for a cowardly buffoon and sordid jester. What hornet-like sting in her sarcasm! What wolf-mouth taunts she hurled at him for his scrupulous timidity! Her bosom with anger was heaving! Her eyes were flashing with rage under the surge of hot anger that swept over her.

Now I know tastes differ and I know this sermon is from the other side of the Atlantic, but I'm afraid it would probably have me in "profuse and harsh laughter" if I was sitting listening to it, if not in open-mouthed disbelief! In my opinion, this is not language for the pulpit – maybe the Elizabethan stage or perhaps Monty Python, but not a twenty-first-century sermon.

Chapter 8   Telling tales

One day Truth walked into town and started preaching in the town square. He was powerful and impressive and had important things to say, and a small crowd gathered. But his appearance was forbidding, his voice loud and strident, and his message blunt and intimidating. So the crowd soon melted away, and after that people avoided him in the street and tried not to catch his eye.

A few days later Parable arrived. He looked very ordinary and not in the least bit impressive, but as he sat next to people in the bars and coffee shops they listened in fascination to the stories he had to tell. Soon the locals were inviting him into their homes to share a meal and to meet their friends.

Truth was upset that everyone was wanting to hear Parable's message while nobody was listening to him, so he sought out Parable and asked him why. Parable took off his battered old hat and put it on Truth, and draped his shabby jacket round Truth's shoulders. He taught him to speak gently and shared some of his stories. Truth was transformed.

Now when Truth comes to town things are very different. His message is the same, but it comes in different clothes. Some people still avoid him, but many welcome him with open arms, and listen gladly to what he has to say.

That story (adapted from Bryan Chapell, *Using Illustrations to Preach with Power*, Crossway Books, 2001) sums up the message of this chapter, and indeed this book. Illustration and story are powerful tools in helping us to get our message across. Of course I'm not saying anything new here. George Herbert wrote in the 17th century, "Exhortations, though earnest, often die with the sermon, especially with country people, which are thick, and heavy, and hard to raise to the point of zeal and fervency, and need a mountain of fire to kindle them; but stories and sayings they will well remember."

I find it hard to believe that this is controversial (though Herbert's description of country folk may well be!) since Scripture itself, and especially the teaching of Jesus, is full of stories and illustrations. If parables are a tool used by Jesus to communicate, and of course by the prophet Nathan in the Old Testament, who am I to ignore them? Yet the use of story in the Bible goes much deeper than that. As many biblical scholars have pointed out, the whole of Scripture is in many ways a story, a "metanarrative" in postmodern jargon, the story of "salvation history" in that of German Old Testament scholars. Will Willimon and Stanley Hauerwas write:

How does God deal with human fear, confusion and paralysis? God tells a story: "I am none other than the God who brought you out of the land of Egypt"... Israel is a people who learn this story by heart and gather regularly to retell it ... Early Christians, interestingly, began not with creedal speculation about the metaphysics of the incarnation, that is, Christology abstracted from the Gospel accounts. They began with stories about Jesus, about those whose lives got caught up in his life.

So every preacher is a storyteller, because our preaching is a retelling of that story, that grand narrative. And our aim should be to tell the story in such a way that those who listen to it can enter into the story and find their place in it, can get caught up in it just as those who first encountered Jesus did. The story does not have to begin "Once upon a time" – indeed, we need to make it clear that this is a true story, one set in history. Yet it does have a fairy-tale ending, of good triumphing over evil, love overcoming hatred and death defeated. Of course, as in all great stories, the path of true love – God's love – never did run smooth, and our preaching should reflect that fact. It's a story of rejection and suffering, in Egypt and Babylon, Jerusalem and the here and now. And yet let us not lose sight of the fact that it does have a happy ending. One of the saddest clergymen I ever met was asked what he preached at Easter. His response: "Easter is God's apology for putting us in this mess." (He actually used a stronger word than "mess", but I'll leave that to your imagination!) This is selling short the biblical story. As preachers we truly have the privilege of proclaiming "The Greatest Story Ever Told". It is a scandal and a sin if we make it boring.

Parables and precepts

I believe our preaching should be patterned on the Bible, that is, that it should contain both story and precept. Jesus gave doctrinal teaching intermingled with illustration: the two underpinned each other. For example, in Matthew 7:1–11, Jesus gives the clear instruction, "Do not judge, or you too will be judged. For in the same way as you judge others, you will be judged, and with the measure you use, it will be measured to you," and follows it immediately with a comic parable about a guy with a huge block of wood in his eye trying to get a speck of sawdust out of someone else's. Then the command to "Ask, seek and knock" is followed by an illustration taken from family life: if earthly parents know not to put stones or snakes in their children's lunchboxes when they ask for bread and fish, "how much more will your Father in heaven give good gifts to those who ask him!" This is also the broader pattern of the Bible, which includes Paul's letters (which are largely precept) alongside the narratives of the Gospels and Acts. The Old Testament likewise puts narrative and precept together, even in the first five books, the Torah. In our teaching, then, let us tell stories but also explain them; give instruction but season it with illustration. We need to keep a balance of parable and precept. Barbara Brown Taylor provides a good example of how not to do it:

> I listened to an Easter sermon once in which the preacher stood up in front of a church full of people hungry for good news and told us Easter bunny jokes,

one after another. He never met our eyes. He looked up at the light fixtures as he delivered his punch lines, never noticing how we laughed less each time. Finally he said something about how Easter was God's joke on death and we should all laugh more. Then he said *Amen* and sat down. I have never in my life wished so badly for pulpit police. I wanted someone with a badge to go up and arrest that guy, slap some handcuffs on him, and lead him away.

The fact is, the story form appeals more to the right-brained, those who prefer intuition and language over doctrine and logic, and many such people sit in our pews. For them we need to include anecdote and illustration. But precepts are favoured by the left-brainers out there, and they need feeding, too. If we provide a varied and balanced diet, everyone gets fed.

Should you buy my book?

If our sermons are going to be liberally sprinkled with illustration, more than just a joke at the start or an application at the end, how do we keep on finding appropriate material? The first thing to say is that "illustration" is much more than simply stories: the brief example from Jesus' teaching quoted above brings that out. It can include all kinds of similes, metaphors, quotations and word pictures, as well as practical applications. An illustration is anything that illustrates, that is, sheds light on the point we're making, and this may not include stories as such at all. What we're looking for is anything that will help to clarify or bring home our point for our listeners, and that may be from books, television, films, the internet or – best of all – daily life.

How we go about finding the illustrations for a particular sermon is very much a matter of individual preference. Some preachers I've read are unbelievably organised, starting to gather illustrations for specific sermons literally months in advance, with suspension files all ready for each talk. To be honest, I don't even know what I'm going to be preaching on that far in advance, and I'm certainly not thinking about that sermon when I've got one or two to deliver this coming Sunday! But it is essential to build up a stock of material from which to draw, and although each of us will have to do the spadework for ourselves, I suggest that a good way of building up such a store is to:

- Collect
- File
- Use.

First of all, **collect** as much as you can. There are loads of books out there to help you get started, so why reinvent the wheel? I've listed some (including my own) at the back under "For further reading". There are always new ones coming out and others going out of print, so keep looking in Christian bookshops (and indeed the Humour section in secular bookshops) to see what's new. They obviously vary in quality and usefulness: my personal test is to randomly read two or three pages in the bookshop, and if there's nothing that grabs me at all, I'll put the book back. If there's something there I can use, I'll buy it, on the assumption that there are bound to be other things on the pages I haven't looked at (it doesn't always work).

The internet can be an invaluable source of sermon illustrations. In addition to the innumerable jokes flying round by e-mail, many of which are unrepeatable in church, but some of which are usable, there is also an increasing number of internet sites which offer illustrations for preachers. Again I've included some sites in the "For further reading" section at the back. I have to say that I haven't used them myself, though they have been recommended to me by others whose ministry I respect. The internet search engines can also be extremely useful ways of finding material that you can't find elsewhere. If you've never used these, engines such as Google or Copernic can be downloaded free of charge, and will search thousands of sites in seconds.

The best material isn't always handed to us on a plate, however. As I read newspapers, magazines and books, I'm always on the lookout for quotable quotes and useful illustrations. It's amazing how much there is. One source I have personally found particularly fruitful is the news magazine, *The Week*. This weekly digest of world news, sport, the arts and business regularly has useful little snippets (and no, I'm not on commission). To give a couple of examples, I read there last week that 46% of Britons would lie about their income to pay less tax, 60% would steal office stationery, 66% would travel by train without a ticket and 36% would park in a disabled parking space. That's a great quote for a sermon on the Commandments.

And the week before Easter 2003 I read the following story, headed "Waiter's unusual donation":

> A waiter at a hotel in Hawaii has been named employee of the year after donating a kidney to a regular customer. Walter Nishioka, 70, a local businessman, was seriously ill with kidney disease and had been told that he needed a transplant urgently. But doctors could not find him a donor – until Jose Rocasa, 52, a waiter at the Radisson Prince Kuhio on Waikiki Beach, offered one of his own. Nishioka had eaten brunch at the hotel every Wednesday for the past 22 years, and had always been a generous tipper. Rocasa's boss described him as "a server who became a saviour".

What a gift for Maundy Thursday, when we remember the Saviour who became a server!

There's no point in collecting the material if we don't know where to find it again: we really do need to **file** it somehow. I heard author Philip Yancey say that he files everything on a computer index, so that he can search quickly in a variety of different ways: by topic, sub-topic, or even individual word. I'm more old-fashioned (and I don't employ a research assistant) so my references are on 6" x 4" index cards, written out in full if they're short, or as a one-line description and location if they're longer, filed under topics such as *Abortion, Abraham, Absent-minded vicar, Abuse* and *Academics* (to quote the first cards in my system). The only problem is remembering where I've filed a particular story, but I can add a note on another card if necessary (for instance, filing the statistics reproduced above under *Commandments*, but with a cross-referencing note on the card for *Lying*).

Then we need to remember to look in our card index when we are preparing our sermon, and **use** the material we've gathered. The great thing is, though, that we're gradually building up a store that will last a lifetime, and that can provide us with thought-provoking inspiration if we're struggling with a particular sermon. (Incidentally, I also have a card for each book of the Bible.) It is important to make a note when we use something, so that we don't tell the same joke three Christmases in a row. The second time people will laugh out of politeness; the third time they'll laugh *at* us! Three other warnings:

- Be real
- Be relevant
- Be ruthless.

First, be **real**. I ignore scores of sermon illustrations because they're just not me. I can't tell a story about American football, for instance, because I just don't understand it. If I quote from Shakespeare or refer to *Eastenders*, I'll confess at the start that I don't really know much about either, because I've only occasionally dipped my toe into both, and I could get some significant fact completely wrong. But there's nothing more real than a story from my own experience. A Norwegian reviewer of my collection of sermon illustrations put it bluntly, "Just the book's subtitle is enough to create scepticism about the whole venture: '247 sparkling stories from life for preachers and teachers'. How doubtful is this for homileticians? Shouldn't a preacher get his good illustrations from his own experience?" Thanks for that! (Though the reviewer did acknowledge that the book could be useful when you're really desperate.) He's right, of course: ideally, we want to illustrate from our own experience, and best of all from our common experience, as Jesus did: "Why do you worry about clothes? See how the lilies of the field grow... " (Matthew 6:28); "Jesus began to speak to the crowd about John: 'What did you go out into the desert to see? A reed swayed by the wind?' " (Matthew 11:7). That was of course also Paul's approach in the meeting of the Areopagus: "Men of Athens! I see that in every way you are very religious. For as I walked around and looked carefully at your objects of worship, I even found an altar with this inscription: TO AN UNKNOWN GOD. Now what you worship as something unknown I am going to proclaim to you" (Acts 17:22–23).

This means that we only use material that's **relevant**. Genuinely relevant to the sermon, first of all. We mustn't be like the clergyman in a cartoon from *Leadership* magazine who is praying, "And Father, I ask thee now for a good text to accompany this fantastic joke." The illustrations we use are the servants of the message, not its master. We must therefore think long and hard – perhaps longer and harder than we tend to do – about how the stories we use will be heard by our listeners. Experience shows that what we say, let alone what we intend to say, is not always what people hear! And when it is so easy for our congregation to get the wrong end of the stick, if we tell an ambiguous story, or even one that goes off at a tangent, we set ourselves up for a fall.

Take for instance the well-known tale of the tardy

oxcart. It's a long story, but in a nutshell it's about a farmer and son on their way to market. The farmer is in no hurry, much to the son's frustration, and the journey seems to take forever. But when they finally reach the city which is their destination, they discover that it's a wasteland, for the city is Hiroshima. Now apart from the question of whether the story is true, what does it actually say? Don't hurry, or you might end up dead? Hardly a biblical message, and arguably not even true – if they'd started out in Hiroshima the reverse would have been the case! More significantly, what does it say – if anything – about God? One interpretation apparently uses it to communicate the faithfulness of God's providence, but since there is no indication that the farmer is a believer or that his slowness is due to his Christian character, indeed, since God is nowhere mentioned in the story, it's by no means an obvious conclusion to draw. At a deeper level, I question whether that application is even justifiable. Precisely the opposite conclusion was drawn by the Protestant divine, Richard Baxter, during the Great Plague of 1665. "At first," he wrote, "so few of the religiouser sort were taken away that (according to the mode of too many such) they began to be puffed up and boast of the great differences which God did make. But quickly after that they all fell alike." Not such a positive or encouraging story, but, I suggest, one that is more true to Scripture and experience.

Equally importantly, our illustrations must be relevant to our listeners. Bill Hybels says, "I sometimes joke that one of my goals in ministry is to complete however many years God gives me in ministry without ever using a Spurgeon illustration. Non-Christians (even most Christians today) don't know who Spurgeon was." I can only agree. Quoting from Augustine or Luther might be impressive in college essays, or indeed college chapels, but in most congregations it means nothing. Unless of course it's a real humdinger of a quote, in which case the point is the quote itself, not the person who said it ("A Christian should be a hallelujah from head to foot!" – Augustine). This poses a huge challenge to us, because society is perhaps more fragmented into preference groups than ever before. To go back to *Eastenders*, even if we do watch it regularly and quote from it in our sermons, we can't assume that all our congregation watch it. If they are typical of the population at large, most of them don't. The same is true of all aspects of popular culture: newspapers, sport, films, etc. We can't simply quote a scene from the latest blockbuster and assume people have seen it. Everything needs to be explained. For instance, when I preached a sermon mentioning Harry Potter, I had to explain who Lord Voldemort was; indeed, who Harry Potter was! We cannot take anything for granted if we truly want to communicate with everybody.

At the same time, we also need to be **ruthless** in cutting anything we are uncertain about or which is potentially hurtful. This includes anything which may not be true, a subject I'll discuss at length in the next chapter, "Lying in the pulpit". In brief, it amazes me how many preachers are willing to use illustrations which are demonstrably false. For instance, an otherwise excellent collection of stories for preachers includes one which tells how Albrecht Dürer's brother supposedly worked down a mine to earn enough money to support Albrecht as he studied painting. The story goes on to identify this brother as the owner of the famous praying hands. The problem is that we know a lot about Dürer's life, and this story simply isn't true. It's a made-up legend (also found in a variant form which makes the hands belong to Dürer's friend, Hans the goldsmith). What does that do for our credibility? But as I said, much more on that in the next chapter.

We should also reject anything which breaches confidentiality: we should not share publicly something which we have been told in confidence. All too many speakers' families sit there during the sermon worrying what new revelation about their private life the preacher is going to divulge this morning! But if we really want to include an illustration from our lives which involves someone else, there are ways to ensure we don't breach confidentiality. One, obviously, is to ask permission; another is to so disguise the individuals concerned that nobody could work out who they are (changing their gender is a good ploy). I also don't think there is a problem if we are certain that nobody present could possibly know the person concerned, though we do have to be careful that we don't leave our congregation afraid to share anything with us in case we might tell the whole world in some future sermon. And of course it is much more acceptable to talk about others anonymously if we are putting them in a positive light rather than talking about their foibles or failures.

A third area we need to be careful about is causing unnecessary offence by slighting comments about other races or religions. I once sat wincing as a free church preacher sneeringly laid into what he saw as Roman Catholic "errors". Having said that, I do believe that there's a perceptible difference between good-natured laughing and scornful mocking, and I think it is possible to become paranoid about political correctness. Only yesterday in my sermon I told a string of "light bulb" jokes about Quakers, Roman Catholics, TV evangelists and Jehovah's Witnesses. But I ended up with one against Anglicans, my own denomination. Similarly, I will often make jokes against women in my wedding sermons. But I'll make sure I balance them with jokes against men. There are typical gender differences, and I think it's helpful if couples go into marriage with their eyes open to that, rather than blissfully ignorant. And if I can do it with humour, all the better. But we must always bear such issues in mind, do all that we can not to cause offence, and be big enough to apologise if we get it wrong.

See hear!

Illustrations can be visual as well as verbal. I've already made this point in Chapter 5, so I won't labour it here. But remember that we supposedly retain only 10% of what we hear but 30% of what we see. So let's use images and objects in our preaching, following God's example:

> The word of the Lord came to me: "What do you see, Jeremiah?"
>
> "I see the branch of an almond tree," I replied.
>
> The Lord said to me, "You have seen correctly, for I am watching to see that my word is fulfilled."
>
> The word of the Lord came to me again: "What do you see?"

"I see a boiling pot, tilting away from the north,"
I answered.

The Lord said to me, "From the north disaster will
be poured out on all who live in the land."

(Jeremiah 1:11–14; cf. Amos 7:7–8; 8:1–2)

From my own experience, I remember a visiting
preacher speaking on Philippians 2:20, "Our citizenship is
in heaven." She explained about Philippi's status as a
Roman colony and, to illustrate, held up her UK passport.
It helped me grasp the point far more clearly than if she'd
just talked about citizenship. Of course we have to beware
of gimmickry – using an object just for the sake of it. That
can actually distract. But a well-used object really can help
to drive our point home.

The same is true of pictures. Illustrations on OHP,
PowerPoint or even old-fashioned card can be a useful aid
to concentration, understanding and learning. Describing
the splendour of Herod's palaces in a picture made of
words can be inspiring; a photograph of the grandeur of
Herodium can stick in the mind for years. Even something
as simple and essentially verbal as putting up quotations
can help people mark, learn and inwardly digest what
we're trying to communicate. The same is true of putting
up our headings, though once again I'd underline the fact
that our aim should not be to get people to learn
"Acceptance, Belonging and Commitment" as much as
what those things mean in their everyday lives.

In short: be creative! Be imaginative! And use every
means possible to help the word of God to impact people's
hearts, minds and lives.

Chapter 9   Lying in the pulpit

Lie? In the pulpit? Who would ever do such a thing? Not me! But in this chapter we will see how easy it is to fall short of preaching the truth, the whole truth and nothing but the truth. We'll look at a series of possible pitfalls:

- Making things up and pretending they're true
- Getting our facts wrong
- Exaggerating
- Failing to practise what we preach
- Using ourselves as role models.

The Ugandan church leader Festo Kivengere used to tell the story of how he had a row with his wife just before he was due to speak at a meeting. He stormed out of the house and tried to calm himself down on the way. But the Holy Spirit spoke to him, saying, "Go back and pray with your wife." He argued that he was due to speak in 20 minutes' time; he would be reconciled with his wife afterwards. "OK," he heard the Lord say. "You go and preach, and I'll stay at home with your wife." He had to turn round, go back and apologise to his wife, and only then could he preach with conviction and integrity.

Integrity is the subject of this chapter. As preachers

we need to be able to stand before our listeners with integrity. People expect us to practise what we preach and preach what we practise. We know, however, that that isn't always the case. One famous TV evangelist is caught with a prostitute in a motel room; another is imprisoned for fraud. A leading evangelical preacher resigns over a relationship with another man. A flagship alternative service is closed down amidst reports of scandalous behaviour by its leader. These are just a few of the very public scandals that have rocked the church in recent years. But even as we shake our heads at these high-profile falls from grace, if we're honest we have to acknowledge that dishonesty happens in less flagrant, more subtle forms, even in our own preaching.

Poetic licence – or a lie?

One form of dishonesty is the technique of putting oneself into a story for greater effect. I have a published collection of humorous stories for preachers where the author has done this repeatedly. If you don't know what I'm talking about, let me illustrate. I once attended a preaching conference in which one of the speakers, a powerful Bible preacher and a delightful man, told a funny story. He told us how his plane had hit some bad turbulence on the flight over from the United States. People were upset, people were panicking, and, because the stewardess had noticed that he was reading the Bible, she asked him if he was a pastor. When he acknowledged that he was, she asked him whether he couldn't do something to calm people down. "Do something religious," she said. So he told us that he went to the front of the cabin and called for everyone's attention, and then ... took up a collection. The story went down well: people laughed, even though many of them must have heard it before – it's one of those golden oldies that's been circulating for years. However, one of my fellow delegates was fuming when we had lunch together. "So now it's OK to lie from the pulpit, is it?" was his question. Although it hadn't struck me that way before, I took his point. If we tell stories that are manifestly untrue in a way that makes it sound as if they are true, we will sow a seed of doubt in the minds of our listeners that the other "true" stories we tell are equally fictitious. In the long run, this will undermine our credibility, and therefore our preaching. Stories which are presented as our own experience should genuinely be our own experience, not someone else's story with the names switched.

A potentially more serious example of this is if we put ourselves into a powerful and dramatic testimony. Back in my university days, the Christian Union had an evangelistic speaker every Sunday night, so regular attenders heard the gospel presented by a whole host of speakers. One particular preacher described how a young man walked into a church, strode up to the altar at the east end and spat on the cross. Then, after a pause for dramatic effect, he declared, "I was that man!" It was stirring stuff. But on the way out a friend expressed his misgivings. "It's funny," he said, "but that's the third different speaker I've heard tell that story – and one of them was a bishop! Did loads of young men go around spitting on crosses, or have some of them made it up?" I didn't know the answer then, and I still don't now, but it highlights the fact that our testimonies must be genuine, honest and true, or some day we will surely be found out. And our credibility will be in tatters.

There are, however, other ways of misleading people that are done with the best of intentions but run the risk of equally negative consequences. Let me again illustrate with an example. Years ago, a lay reader in one of the churches I've attended told a story about the addictive power of possessions. She described how, as the Titanic went down, a wealthy lady was bobbing in the water, clinging onto her jewellery box. A lifeboat pulled alongside her and she was told to let go of the box and pull herself on board. She refused, saying that she had to bring the box with her. After further fruitless attempts to persuade her, the boat's crew reluctantly moved on and left her in the water, for they couldn't afford to take the heavy, bulky box as well. That was the last anyone ever saw of the woman: by clinging onto her worldly wealth she forfeited her life. After the service I congratulated the preacher and said, "That was a great story! Where did you get it from?" She replied, "I made it up!" I was horrified. You can't make up a story like that which pretends to be historical! To be blunt, that's lying in the pulpit. Having said that, I am not for a moment suggesting that we should not make up stories. After all, Jesus did it all the time: we call them parables. It seems to me that that is the way to use a story like this. Tell the story as a parable: "A wealthy woman was once on her way from Liverpool to New York aboard a mighty cruise ship..." You could also preface the illustration with a qualifying phrase such as "The story is told that..." But don't tie the event to an actual historical event – or an actual ship!

The reason is that people listen and respond differently to a made-up story on the one hand and an example or illustration from life on the other. Either can be used to great effect in a sermon, but it must be made clear into which category the particular illustration falls. If they think that you're telling a made-up story, they will hear it one way; if they know that this actually happened, it will have a different kind of impact. This is why I'm careful about using the terms "Bible story" or "story from the Bible". I use those terms all the time, often without thinking, but I am very conscious that to some people in the congregation it may give the impression that a "story" is not something that actually happened. In the case of the parable of the prodigal son, that's fine. When I'm preaching about David and Goliath or Jesus walking on the water, however, I want people to know that I regard this as an actual historical event. So I will refer to them as "episodes" or "events" as well as "stories", in order to drive the point home. There's a good illustration of this in (of all places) the Monty Python film *Life of Brian*. A teacher (who is, incidentally, clearly differentiated from Jesus) starts telling the crowd a story: "There was this man, and he had two servants..." At that point he's interrupted by the question, "What were they called?" "I don't know," he answers, then tries to carry on, "... and he gave them some talents." The questioner then appeals to the crowd, "He doesn't know what they were called!" So the storyteller foolishly attempts to remedy the situation, "Oh, they were called Simon and Adrian." His tormentor seizes on this, "You said you didn't know." And turning triumphantly to the crowd, he says, "He's making it up as he goes along!" Precisely! The point of parables is that they were – and are

– made-up stories. The teacher's denial in the film, "No, I'm not!" is a huge mistake (though possibly not as damaging to his cause as his next comment, "Oh wait a minute, were there three?"). If people know that what they are hearing is fiction, they will treat it as such. Names don't matter. If, however, they have been led to believe they are hearing fact, they process it another way, and getting names wrong can matter very much. Woe to the preacher who confuses the two categories!

Not deceptive but defective

Another pitfall for the unwary preacher is our fallible memory. It's arguable whether this is lying, because there is genuinely no intent to deceive. But it can be equally damaging to our integrity, because if there is someone present who knows the true story, it will, as in all these cases, undermine our credibility and our authority. Having a spouse in the congregation is a good remedy for this flaw. I was once speaking at a houseparty and quoted an example from our own church. Afterwards my wife asked me who I had been talking about, and when I told her, put me right. I had misremembered precisely what had happened and given a misleading version of events. As far as possible, we need to check our facts beforehand, and if we're unsure about the details, be upfront about it.

I have, for example, read in an otherwise excellent book of sermon illustrations a distorted version of the story of Maximilian Kolbe. He was a Polish priest who freely offered his life in exchange for that of another prisoner at Auschwitz in 1941. It is an incredibly powerful and moving testimony of the power of love over hatred and hope over despair, and one that every preacher should have in his or her library. Unfortunately the author of this particular book, who had actually visited Auschwitz, described Kolbe as being hanged, when in fact he died a lingering death in an underground bunker. Does that really matter? I think it does. Because if we tell our congregation that Kolbe's death by hanging was an amazing example of sacrificial love, and they subsequently discover from another source that he wasn't actually hanged, they may well discount the whole story as unreliable, and thus no longer be moved by the example of his sacrifice.

Tall tales

Yet another way in which we lie in the pulpit, deliberately or more often unintentionally, is by exaggeration. Public speakers, including preachers, can be just as unreliable as fishermen when telling tales of past events. Minor victories over temptation become great spiritual triumphs; small disagreements turn into catastrophic schisms; questions from one or two people become, "Many people have asked me ... " As often as not it's our defective memory at work again – we don't set out to deceive. Having said that, it is sometimes also for effect, to spice up a story or to drive a point home. I think for example of a preacher I heard recently who described Paul as having "probably the greatest mind in the ancient world". That little word "probably" might be enough to rescue the situation, but given the likes of Plato, Socrates and Aristotle, it's a bold claim to make, and I would say it's an exaggeration.

Or there was the time not long ago when I was preaching on Jesus as the Prince of Peace. I remembered a colleague telling me some years ago of the remarkable situation at his church, where one of the two churchwardens was a former SS officer and the other a Jewess who had escaped the Nazi death camps, her camp number still tattooed on her arm. It seemed the perfect illustration, but as it was some years since I'd last used it, I thought I'd better check the details. It was a good thing I did. They weren't churchwardens but lay readers, and, more to the point, the lady had not been imprisoned in the camps, but had fled to this country before the war. It is so easy to exaggerate without being aware that we're doing it. The danger is that our reputation for truthfulness and trustworthiness is fatally compromised, and we must do all that we can to avoid it.

Preaching and practising

So far we have looked at specific instances of communication. They are relatively easy to identify and, to a greater or lesser extent, to guard against. A much broader, much more difficult and arguably much more significant issue is the relationship between what we say and what we do. Is there an integrity between our sermons and our lives? That is the theme of the rest of this chapter. It seems to me that there are three interrelated issues here, which are best summed up by three questions: What right do I have as a preacher to tell anyone else how to live? Do others have the right to expect me to maintain higher moral and ethical standards than the rest of the congregation? Is it right to use my own experience in sermon illustrations?

First, then, what right does a preacher have to tell anyone else how to live? The seventeenth-century writer John Selden wrote in his book of *Table Talk*, "Preachers say, 'Do as I say, not as I do.' But if the physician had the same disease upon him that I have, and he should bid me do one thing, and himself do quite another, could I believe him?" He seems to have a point, but reflection shows the comparison to be unfair. Assuming, as I have throughout this book, that the preacher is keen to be true to the Bible and to reflect its perspective, he or she should surely be preaching to him- or herself as much as to the congregation. Whether in the pulpit or out of it, I must never lose sight of the fact that I am as much a sinner saved by grace as the people I am addressing, and always will be. As James says specifically about those who teach, "We all stumble in many ways" (James 3:2). The prescription for the disease is consequently the same, even if we may have been under treatment for longer and may even be responding well to it. It is so easy to forget this point, particularly if other people tend to put us on a pedestal. That can be very flattering. As Calvin Miller says, "Pulpits strangle all the natural Pastor Jekyll from our lives and change us into a saintly, seminary Dr. Hyde, M.Div., PhD." Nonetheless, it's a temptation we must avoid, for if the congregation puts us on a pedestal, sooner or later they will see our feet of clay.

So we all stumble and will often find ourselves falling short of the message we preach, but at the same time I trust that we want to live up to it and try to live up to it. It is not, as Selden suggests, that we present one way of life to the congregation but live by a different standard ourselves. Rather, we hold up the ideal, knowing that none of us will attain it in this life, but seeking to pursue it day by day. As Antoine de Saint-Exupéry put it: "Ideals are like the stars; we may not be able to reach them, but we set our course by them." Or, as Paul said: "Not that I have already obtained all this, or have already been made perfect, but I press on to take hold of that for which Christ Jesus took hold of me" (Philippians 3:12). I will sometimes say to the congregation as an aside during the sermon, "I'm preaching to myself here!" In sum, it's not so much that we say, "Do as I say, not as I do," as that we say, "Try to do as I say, as I am trying to myself."

It is quite a different matter, however, if in a sermon I exhort others to an attitude or to behaviour which I have no intention of upholding in my own personal life. To me that is blatant hypocrisy, which ought to disqualify one from preaching. Of course it does unfortunately happen. In his book on churches that abuse, Ken Blue writes, "Another pastor I knew made much of the fact that he never used the church's envelopes or stamps to mail his personal letters. He stated this to me on at least three occasions. This same man was later fired for stealing cash from the offering plates, which were stored in his office between services." These are the kind of episodes which make headlines in the papers when they are uncovered. The vicar who thunders against adultery while carrying on an affair. The pastor who urges honesty from the pulpit but is then found to have lied about his qualifications. The lay preacher who runs his company by totally different standards from the ones he upholds in his sermons. To be fair, preachers who are living like this will not be saying in a sermon, "Do as I say, not as I do," because they will be keeping quiet from the congregation what it is they are doing. But the demand for integrity is nonetheless laid on us all, not only by Scripture and by our congregations, but also, ironically, by the secular press, who are very quick to point out hypocrisy in the pulpit.

This brings me to the second question. I acknowledge that I am just as much of a sinner as the rest of the people of God, and am preaching as much to myself as I am to them. Why, then, do others expect me to maintain higher moral and ethical standards than them? Samuel Butler wrote: "The clergyman is expected to be a kind of human Sunday. Things must not be done in him which are venial in the week-day classes. He is paid for this business of leading a stricter life than other people. It is his *raison d'être*. If his parishioners feel that he does this they approve of him, for they look upon him as their own contribution towards what they deem a holy life. This is why the clergyman is so often called a 'vicar' – he being the person whose vicarious goodness is to stand for that of those entrusted to his charge." Admittedly this was said in a comic novel from the late-nineteenth century, but I suspect it is true in many churches today.

Turning to the Bible for guidance, though we may resent it or find it difficult, Scripture does expect those who teach others to set an example by their high standards of behaviour. For instance, Paul tells Timothy: "Set an example for the believers in speech, in life, in love, in faith and in purity," and goes on to link that charge with preaching: "Until I come, devote yourself to the public reading of Scripture, to preaching and to teaching." The link between personal conduct and preaching is made even more explicitly a few verses later: "Watch your life and doctrine closely. Persevere in them, because if you do, you will save both yourself and your hearers" (1 Timothy 4:12–13, 16). In a different vein, James writes: "Not many of you should presume to be teachers, my brothers, because you know that we who teach will be judged more strictly" (James 3:1). This again implies that a higher standard is expected of those of us who preach. Douglas Moo comments, "One who undertakes to lead others in the faith must be careful that his own life reflects what he is teaching. His greater knowledge brings with it a greater responsibility to live according to that knowledge." In short, then, others do have the right to expect higher standards of conduct from those who preach. Not, as Samuel Butler puts it, as their representative, their contribution towards a holy life. But rather, as Peter says of church leaders, as "examples to the flock" (1 Peter 5:3).

Me, myself, I

This brings me to the third question, namely the debate over whether the preacher should use his or her own experience as a sermon illustration. There is a school of thought which rules this out completely, arguing that this makes the speaker the focus of the talk rather than Christ. At the opposite end of the scale is the Norwegian reviewer mentioned in the previous chapter, who argued that as far as possible we should illustrate our talks with material from our own experience. Where does the right balance lie? It seems to me that it is somewhere between these two extremes. On the one hand, we have a clear biblical mandate to talk about ourselves when we preach, in that the preachers of the Old and New Testaments regularly did so. For example, at the heart of Peter's sermons in Acts is the statement "We are witnesses" (2:32; 3:15; 10:39). Similarly, in Paul's letters the apostle repeatedly spoke about himself and his own experience. There is consequently an excellent precedent for referring to ourselves in our sermons. On the other hand, there is always the danger that in preaching about ourselves we both draw attention to ourselves rather than to God and make ourselves look good. Paul was evidently conscious of this pitfall, in that he frequently included in his personal testimonies unambiguous references to his shortcomings and failings. Thus he described his privilege of seeing the risen Christ in the following terms: "Last of all he appeared to me also, as to one abnormally born" and continued, "For I am the least of the apostles and do not even deserve to be called an apostle, because I persecuted the church of God" (1 Corinthians 15:8–9). This is one way of ensuring that we do not glorify ourselves when we use ourselves as an example: share our flaws and failures, and tell stories about God's goodness towards us rather than about our goodness towards him. Paul again gives us a pattern to follow, when he says, "I will not boast about myself, except about my weaknesses" (2 Corinthians 12:5). This ensures that we do not mount a pedestal, nor allow others to put us there.

There is, what is more, something immensely powerful about confession. Not using the congregation as our therapist, nor misusing candour to disarm our critics, but honestly sharing our struggles and our past mistakes with our fellow Christians. Calvin Miller writes, "Vulnerability opens our audiences like a rose unfolding to light." Care is needed that we don't overdo it, either in the frequency with which we share or in the depth of what we reveal. We also need to keep in mind the whole question of confidentiality, which I have discussed elsewhere. But our reputation for integrity and our credibility as preachers is only enhanced if we share openly with our congregations the reality of our own Christian life.

Chapter 10 Handling hot potatoes

The story is told of a clergyman who was desperate to stir up some enthusiasm in his congregation. Week after week he preached his heart out with very little response, and in despair he said to his wife one Monday morning, "I give up! Next Sunday I'm going to preach on something ridiculous and see if anyone says anything at all. I'll preach on... Oh, I don't know ... I'll preach on riding a bicycle!" And with that he stormed off and slammed the study door.

He hadn't really meant what he said, and as the week went by he continued to muse over what he could choose as a sermon topic that would really make the congregation sit up and take notice. Then it came to him – he would preach on sex! He worked hard, prepared conscientiously, and put together a sermon that he thought should really do the trick. And it worked! People stirred and listened attentively, and after the sermon he had more positive comments at the door than he'd had for ages. His only regret was that his wife hadn't been there to hear it, because she was away for the weekend visiting her elderly mother.

As she arrived back at the station on Sunday evening his wife bumped into a member of the congregation. "Jolly good sermon your husband preached this morning," he said. "Really?" said his wife in surprise, remembering that he was going to preach on riding a bicycle. "I'm amazed! As far as I know he's only done it a couple of times, and one of those he fell off."

Sex is one of those subjects that most preachers tend to fight shy of, despite the fact that the Bible is full of it. Money is another. In this chapter we'll look at a few of the trickier issues that I believe we are called to address from the pulpit, and consider how to do so with integrity, sensitivity and authority.

Sex

Mike Pilavachi writes in his book *Wasteland?* about his amazement as a teenager on first coming across the Song of Songs.

> I decided to read the Bible from Genesis to Revelation. Eventually I finished Ecclesiastes, and after taking some antidepressants turned the page. The title of the next book, Song of Songs, did not give any indication of what was in store. I thought it was a book about singing worship songs. After the first few verses, my eyes were on stalks. I thought, "Who's put this in the book? I don't believe it – someone's spiked my Bible!"

The book is a frank celebration of sexual love, but because the church has found that hard to handle, over the centuries it has regularly been either ignored or explained away. I preached on it at our eight o'clock communion service one Sunday morning (on one of the very few occasions on which the Lectionary offers the chance to preach on Song of Songs) and asked the congregation whether they had ever heard a sermon on the book before. Despite the fact that these were people who had been attending church for years, several agreed that this was indeed a first for them. And even when the book is dusted off and brought out into the light, its message is often spiritualised. For instance, I know of three songs based on it. One, an ancient Graham Kendrick number, quotes 2:10–12, "Come arise my love, my fairest daughter," and applies it to the Second Coming. Two others are based on 2:4, "He brought me to his banqueting table, and his banner over me is love," but both use this as a picture of the believer's intimacy with Jesus. These may well be legitimate applications, but their effect is to undermine, rather than underline, the original message of the book.

Nor is the Song of Songs the only book of the Bible in which sex is featured in a positive light. From Adam and Eve in the garden and the command to "Go forth and multiply," to Paul's instruction in 1 Corinthians Chapter 7 that husbands and wives should not deny each other, Scripture upholds sex as good and a gift from God. Unfortunately the church has rarely preached this message, more often giving the impression that sex is dirty, embarrassing or just plain wrong. Nicky Gumbel quotes the medieval writer Yves of Chartres, who taught that abstinence had to be practised on Thursdays in memory of Jesus' arrest, Fridays in memory of his death, Saturdays in honour of Mary, Sundays because of the resurrection and Mondays out of respect for the faithful departed! Is it a remnant of Greek philosophical thinking, a hangover from the ancient Manichean and Cathar heresies, that is, a tendency to see spirit as good and matter as evil? Or is it that we preachers have focused so much on the biblical prohibition of sex outside marriage that we've neglected to teach on the positive blessing of sex within marriage? Whatever the cause, the remedy for abuse is not disuse but right use, and in a society which is so obsessed with sex but so wilfully ignorant of the maker's instructions that came with the gift, it is up to us preachers to tell our congregations what that means.

Unfortunately, embarrassment or lack of confidence means that we rarely do so. This was brought home to me again recently when I read in a book on preaching from the United States that we should avoid using illustrations which are "graphic, sensational or crude" in their references to sex or violence. The writer goes on, "The story of David's sin with Bathsheba, for instance, should not be told in such a way as to pander to basic interests." And here he shoots himself in the foot, it seems to me, because he reminds us that the Bible itself, especially the Old Testament, is full of graphic and sensational material. Look at Judges Chapter 19, for example, or 2 Samuel Chapter 13, or Ezekiel Chapter 16, to name just a few. These are admittedly particularly hard passages to preach on, but the stories of Samson and David are just as graphic and very much in the mainstream of biblical preaching. What is more, as Phyllis Trible reminds us in her book *Texts of Terror*, even the hard passages are part of the book we acknowledge as Scripture, and we dare not hide from them for ever. I'm not suggesting for a moment that we should be smutty or crude in the pulpit, but at the same time let's not be prudes. Let's avoid being worldly, sure, but let's also avoid the other extreme, being other-worldly!

At the same time, the Old Testament episodes that I've just mentioned provide an important reminder that sex can cause great pain when it is abused, and this is just as true today. We dare not preach with high-flown rhetoric about this wonderful gift from God and ignore the very real suffering among members of our own congregation. We must be sensitive and honest, and speak words of understanding and comfort. We must also remember that there may well be people sitting listening who bear a tremendous load of guilt about the subject because of past or even present actions. As Bill Hybels says in *Mastering Contemporary Preaching*, we need to offer not only the promise of grace but also a rope to help such individuals out of their pit, including practical advice on how to break wrong and harmful patterns of sexual behaviour.

Money

If sex is one topic rarely mentioned in the pulpit, then money is another that many preachers find hard to tackle. It may be because it's considered vulgar to talk about it in our culture; it may be because most preachers are directly or indirectly paid by their congregations, and so fear a charge of self-interest; it may be because we're desperate not to acquire a reputation of always asking for money. Whatever the reason, if we fight shy of talking about money we have to leave out an awful lot of the Bible. At least a dozen of Jesus' parables address the topic of wealth and material goods. Indeed, it's been calculated that around one in every eight verses of the Gospels deals with this subject. Paul, too, spends a lot of time talking about giving. So if we want to be truly biblical preachers, we are going to have to talk about the subject of money. How should we go about it?

The first thing to say is that we should never set out to induce guilt. If those who are in Christ are no longer under condemnation, as Paul assures us, then it is most definitely not the preacher's job to try to make the people in the pews squirm. God loves a *cheerful* giver, Paul says, not a miserable, guilty one. So let us preach generosity. God has been so generous to us, in creating life, sustaining life, and most of all in giving us eternal life. "For you know the grace of our Lord Jesus Christ, that though he was rich, yet for your sakes he became poor, so that you through his poverty might become rich" (2 Corinthians 8:9). In our giving we are therefore simply giving back to God, not out of guilt but out of gratitude. As the Texan industrialist R. G. LeTourneau put it, "The question is not how much of my money I give to God, but rather how much of God's money I keep." Such teaching releases people to give, rather than placing heavy burdens on their shoulders.

This also means that we should focus on biblical principles rather than the church's needs. There is a time and a place to inform people about figures and budgets, and I firmly believe we should give as many people as possible as much information as possible so that everyone in the church is well informed. But I suggest that the sermon is not normally the place for that. Rather, in the sermon we lay out before people what the Scriptures say about money and about giving. How Jesus warns of the seductive dangers of wealth and tells us to use our money for the kingdom. How he praises the example of the widow who gives her mite and how the rich young man goes away sorrowful. How the measure we use will be the measure with which we are repaid, and so on. Here Paul provides an excellent role model. In 2 Corinthians Chapters 8 and 9 he could have majored on the needs of the church in Jerusalem, the importance of his collection and the good it would do. Instead he chose to focus on the blessings the Corinthians had already received from God and the further blessings they would receive if they continued to give.

Paul also reminds us that our giving should be planned: "On the first day of every week, each one of you should set aside a sum of money in keeping with his income, saving it up, so that when I come no collections will have to be made" (1 Corinthians 16:2). In the same way, I believe that our teaching on giving should be planned so that it forms a regular part of our preaching programme, rather than only when funds are running low or we have a particular project to finance. I try to make sure that there is at least one sermon on money and giving every year, as part of a broader series on a particular book of the Bible or a thematic series on discipleship. As I have already mentioned, because the subject of wealth and our handling of it crops up so often in Scripture, especially in the New Testament, it is not difficult for this to happen perfectly naturally. Looking back over my own preaching programme, I have most recently included sermons on giving in a series on the nature of the church as reflected in Acts 2:42–47 and in a series from Mark's Gospel, on the rich young man.

Another important principle in this context is the need to be real. In all our preparation we should be thinking about our specific audience and their specific situation, and this is particularly significant when preaching about money. Appropriate illustration is crucial, both to encourage and to challenge. The question of whether we should use ourselves as examples is, however, particularly tricky. If I tell the congregation what percentage I give, or how God has honoured my sacrificial giving, I risk being perceived as trying to make myself look good. But if I never refer to my own giving, people may wonder whether I am willing to practise what I preach. It's a tough one to call, and each of us is going to have to make up our own minds before God.

Finally, when preaching about such sensitive subjects as money and sex, we should definitely make use of humour. It can do a wonderful job of defusing tension and helping people to cope with what are for many, let's be honest, difficult and personal subjects. Of course it has to be appropriate humour, especially in the area of sex, and personally I don't think that jokes about Jews or Scotsmen being mean are helpful. But there are lots of good, clean jokes about giving and yes, even about sex out there, and if I can get people laughing, they will relax and be more open to the serious things I want to say. Here's one for starters:

A vicar stopped to ask a group of teenagers sitting on the grass outside the church what they were doing.

"Oh nothing really," one lad answered. "We were just seeing who could tell the biggest lie about our sex lives."

"Boys, boys!" the vicar said. "When I was your age I never even used to think about such things."

"You win, vicar!" they chorused.

Issues

If our preaching is going to be relevant to everyday life, I believe that there are times when we must tackle controversial contemporary issues, either as the specific subject of a sermon, or in the context of a Bible passage. Some such issues feature in the Bible: remarriage after divorce, for instance, or the place of the land of Israel in God's promises. Although we could pass over them in silence, being true to Scripture means that a time will come when we have to bite the bullet and preach on them. Other topics crop up in debates in the wider church – abortion, euthanasia, freemasonry or party politics, to name a few – and although it takes a conscious decision to include them in our preaching programme, I suggest that we are letting our congregation down if we do not at some point try to bring a biblical perspective to bear on them.

Sometimes we might even feel we have to cancel our published sermon topic and address a subject that is on everyone's minds at the time, such as many preachers did when the tsunami struck South Asia on Boxing Day 2004 or after the attack on the World Trade Center on September 11th, 2001. Because emotions are often raw at such a time and people may well have very different attitudes to such events, we need to be particularly sensitive, and can never assume that our listeners will think as we do. I know of one minister whose relationship with his congregation broke down over some ill-advised remarks he made on just such an occasion.

It is, of course, much safer all round if we never touch on such difficult issues. We avoid the risk of upsetting anyone or splitting the congregation, and keep clear of the thin ice we know we will be skating on. By sticking to expressing our opinions only on matters of biblical exegesis – where we are usually the only expert in town – we can stay in our comfort zone and save ourselves a lot of hard work in preparation. But is that right? To me it's like pulling up the drawbridge between the biblical world and the real world we all live in. We are leaving our congregation to find their way through the moral maze without a guide, and abandoning the ethical field to the pundits and columnists of the secular media. The upshot may well be that the opinions of our congregation will be formed without any reference to what the Bible or indeed the church has to say on the subject.

I know I'm being provocative here, and I know too that many people avoid these sensitive issues for good and laudable reasons, namely a desire not to oversimplify complex questions or to seek to impose their own views on their congregation. But I believe it is possible to tackle such matters in an even-handed way which helps people to make up their own minds, as long as we take various steps to clarify questions of authority, to ensure balance and to avoid prejudice.

The first and perhaps most important thing is to

make it very clear where authority lies in such matters. I personally attach supreme authority to the Bible as the only sure and trustworthy source of God's revelation. But the Bible still needs to be interpreted, and there's the rub. There are some issues on which the Bible says nothing, and others on which different texts seem to say different things. That's not to say that this is always the case. Someone once said to the American humorist Will Rogers, "The Bible troubles me because there are parts of it I just don't understand." Rogers replied, "It troubles me because there are parts of it that I do understand!" But in disputed matters we need to be entirely clear with the congregation that Christians do disagree over this particular issue, and without necessarily going into a lot of detail outline the opinions on each side. If we declare at this point what our own view is, it's important that we say with Paul, "I say this (I, not the Lord)..." (1 Corinthians 7:12), and emphasise that ultimate biblical authority does not rest with us! In some cases, I think that we should not express our personal opinion at all. I heard of one pastor preaching at election time who took as his text Proverbs 4:27: "Do not swerve to the right or the left; keep your foot from evil," and so left his congregation with the strong impression that they should vote Liberal Democrat! I think it's perfectly right and good that in our preaching we should encourage people to bring their faith into their politics and to reflect as Christians on which way to vote. I have indeed done so myself. But I don't think it is for us as preachers to suggest which party to vote for.

This brings me to the need for balance. There are various ways of ensuring that people really do get a clear picture of both sides of the argument. The simplest is to set them out verbally or visually, using an OHP, PowerPoint slide or a handout. We might think about having two speakers, one setting out each side of the case. This worked effectively in a church that was divided over whether or not it was permissible for a church leader to be a freemason. At an evening service, when there was no pressure of time, there were two speakers, one after the other, each setting out one side of the argument, then briefly responding to what they had heard. The whole thing was done with dignity and respect, and produced a lot more light than heat. In such a context it is particularly helpful if there is an opportunity for comments and questions. As I mentioned in a previous chapter, I adopted this approach in the case of a sermon setting out why I believed it was wrong for this country to go to war with Iraq. I made it clear that I was well aware that not everybody shared this view, and stated that I wanted to give other people the chance to put their point of view at the end. To my surprise, nobody did, and several people thanked me for putting into words what they felt. I can't guarantee we'll always be so fortunate!

Finally, in line with what I said earlier about the range of possible interpretations of the Bible, we should not fight shy of tackling popular prejudice. At the time of writing, the question of the ordination of practising gay clergy is dividing the Anglican Church. I personally take a conservative stance on the matter, based on my reading of the Bible, but I was nonetheless horrified to read the result of a recent poll which said that only 69% of churchgoers were happy for *celibate* homosexuals to be ordained. Whatever the issue under discussion, we must be willing to expose prejudice and hypocrisy when we come across it. There were certainly a few prejudices on show when I spoke on a Christian view of Europe, but they can pop up in all sorts of contexts. When tackling contemporary issues in our preaching, as I would strongly encourage you to do, the aim is, as Paul says, to "demolish arguments and every pretension that sets itself up against the knowledge of God, and [to] take captive every thought to make it obedient to Christ" (2 Corinthians 10:5).

Conclusion

I preached my first sermon at the age of 16, when my dad discovered one Saturday morning that he was too ill to make it into the pulpit the next day. Somehow the *Evening Standard* found out, and I ended up on page three. I still remember how terrifying, and yet at the same time how exhilarating, that first sermon was.

Yes, preaching can be terrifying and exhilarating. Terrifying for all sorts of reasons, some good and some not so good. It is an awesome privilege to seek to bring God's word – not just my words, but *God's* word – to his people. It is nerve-racking to preach the challenging and prophetic messages which Scripture sometimes demands of us. (On such occasions Walter Brueggemann says: "Get down and hide behind the text. You can peek out from behind the text and say, 'It's not me saying this. It's the text!'") It's scary to feel the expectation of the congregation upon us, not only to feed them and instruct them but perhaps also to entertain them. I thank God for the blessed Eutychus, who showed us in Acts 20:9 that even Paul could send people to sleep with his preaching! Incidentally, I thank God, too, for 2 Peter 3:16, which reveals that not even Peter could understand some of the things in Paul's letters. Preaching is an awesome business:

"Not many of you should presume to be teachers, my brothers, because you know that we who teach will be judged more strictly" (James 3:1).

Yet preaching is, and should be, exhilarating as well. It is such a privilege and a joy to be able to teach God's people, to expound God's word and to use the gifts God has given us. I love the image Will Willimon uses: "The preacher is the one who, in service to the church, strikes the rock and brings forth water in dry places. Whenever we gather on Sunday, the question is still, 'Is the Lord among us or not?' And every Sunday the preacher strikes the rock and there is water. The Lord is with us." By ourselves we cannot produce the water, we cannot assuage the people's thirst, but with the help of the Holy Spirit, we can hit the right spot in the rock so that the water gushes forth. What an honour! What a blessing! No wonder Martin Lloyd-Jones once said, "To me the work of preaching is the highest and the greatest and the most glorious calling to which anyone can ever be called." Even if we may not feel we are in the same league as Dr Lloyd-Jones, I trust that we, too, are conscious of the glory and privilege of our calling to preach.

My dad died as I was writing this book. As a preacher I owe him a lot, not because I preach like him (I don't) but because of the encouragement he gave me, the confidence he showed in me, and the love of preaching he passed on to me. That's a great legacy to leave behind. And so I want to end this book by reminding us all of the obligation and opportunity we have to pass the torch on to a new generation of preachers, lay and ordained. Let us look for those in our congregations who may be willing and able to try out their gift, and give them opportunities to do so. Let us teach them and train them (or if necessary, gently but firmly discourage them) and pass on to them what we have learned. And let us always be willing to learn more ourselves, to go on growing in our insight and understanding as to what it means to be a preacher of the kingdom.

> Each of you has been blessed with one of God's many wonderful gifts to be used in the service of others. So use your gift well. If you have the gift of speaking, preach God's message. If you have the gift of helping others, do it with the strength that God supplies. Everything should be done in a way that will bring honour to God because of Jesus Christ, who is glorious and powerful for ever. Amen.
>
> (1 Peter 4:10–11, CEV)

For further reading

This is by no means an exhaustive list, but simply reflects a few of the resources which I myself have found useful.

Books on preaching

D. A. Carson, *Exegetical Fallacies* (Baker Book House, 1984)

Bill Hybels, Stuart Briscoe and Haddon Robinson, *Mastering Contemporary Preaching* (Multnomah Press, 1989, out of print)

Calvin Miller, *Spirit, Word and Story* (Baker Books, 1989); *The Empowered Communicator* (Broadman and Holman, 1994); *Marketplace Preaching* (Baker Books, 1995) and *The Sermon Maker* (Zondervan, 2002)

Haddon W. Robinson, *Biblical Preaching* (Baker Books, 1980); *Biblical Sermons* (Baker Books, 1989) and *Making a Difference in Preaching* (Baker Books, 1999)

Marshall Shelley (ed.), *Changing Lives Through Preaching and Worship: 30 Strategies for Powerful Communication* (Ballantine Books, 1995, out of print)

William H. Willimon, *Peculiar Speech: Preaching to the Baptized* (Eerdmans, 1992) and *The Intrusive Word: Preaching to the Unbaptized* (Eerdmans, 1994)

Books of illustrations

Tony Campolo, *Let Me Tell You a Story* (Word, 2000)

Simon Coupland, *A Dose of Salts* (Monarch, 1997, out of print) and *Spicing Up Your Speaking* (Monarch, 2000).

J. John and Mark Stibbe, *A Box of Delights* (Monarch, 2001); *A Bucket of Surprises* (Monarch, 2002); *A Barrel of Fun* (Monarch, 2003) and *A Bundle of Laughs* (Monarch, 2005)

Graham Twelftree, *Your Point Being* (Monarch, 2003)

Websites for illustrations

www.cybersalt.org

www.bible.org

www.cybercheeze.com/jokes